CRYSTAL GRIDCRAFT

A WITCH'S GUIDE TO SUPERCHARGE YOUR
HEALING CRYSTALS THROUGH GRIDWORK BY
HARNESSING THE POWER OF SACRED
GEOMETRY AND ANCIENT WITCHCRAFT
WISDOM

ESTELLE A. HARPER

How to Get the Most Out of this Book

As a gift to my dear readers, I have created several free resources to help you get the most out of your crystal journey. To get access to these bonuses, scan the QR code below or visit

https://cosmiccompendiums.com/bonus

Here are some of the things you get access to:

Free Bonus # 1: 7-Day Crystal Spell Challenge

Join me as I guide you through a simple process for creating your own crystal spell. This guide includes:

- Daily checklist
- Mindful journaling prompts and questions
- Bite-sized daily actions

Free Bonus # 2: Crystal GridCraft Companion Workbook

Get access to the **60-page** digital workbook for my foundational book on Crystal Grids, including:

- **65** Fill-in-the-blank questions (with an answer key)
- **26** Worksheet questions to plan your crystal grid
- **17** Detailed sacred geometry diagrams
- Full chakra color diagram
- **98** color images of crystals and crystal shapes
- 10 notes sections for your personal notes
- Instructions on how to use the workbook

Free Bonus # 3: All My Future Books

As an email subscriber, you'll be the first to hear about all my new books, and even get a digital copy for free!

- Read my future books for free before they are released
- Give me direct feedback & ideas on future book topics

Free Bonus # 4: My Personal Email

You get access to a direct line of contact to me through my personal email!

- Ask me any questions you have regarding crystal witchcraft
- I personally read and respond to every email I receive
- I'll send you email updates on all things witchy and mystical

And more in the future!

To get access to these bonuses, scan the QR code below or visit

https://cosmiccompendiums.com/bonus

CONTENTS

Introduction   13

PART ONE
THE WONDERS OF CRYSTAL
MAGIC AND CRYSTAL GRIDS

1. A GLIMPSE INTO CRYSTAL MAGIC   23
   Crystals throughout History   23
   Religious Practices and Crystals   36
   Crystals and Witchcraft   43

2. THE SECRETS OF THE UNIVERSE AND
   HOW THEY INFLUENCE CRYSTAL GRIDS   49
   Understanding Sacred Geometry   49
   Sacred Geometry Symbols   53
   Summing Up   72
   Crystal Grids   74

PART TWO
THE ELEMENTS OF A DEEPLY
POWERFUL CRYSTAL GRID

3. HARNESS THE NATURAL FREQUENCIES
   OF COLOR MAGIC   83
   What Is Color Magic?   84
   Crystals and Their Relationship to Chakras   85
   Crystal Color Magic   92

4. DISCOVER THE PHYSICAL
   CHARACTERISTICS THAT ENHANCE
   GRID ENERGY   101
   Crystal Size   101
   Crystal Shapes   105
   Activating Crystal Grids   107

Good Picks for Center Stones   108
Good Picks for Surrounding Stones   122

5. CULTIVATING SYNERGY THROUGH
CRYSTAL COMBINATIONS   129
What Are Crystal Combinations?   129
Factors to Consider When Choosing Crystal
Combinations   131
Alternative Ideas for Choosing Crystal
Combinations   133

6. UPGRADING THE VIBE BY
MAINTAINING AN ENERGETICALLY
SAFE SPACE   147
Personal Ritual Space   149

PART THREE
THE FOUNDATION OF ALL
CRYSTAL GRIDS

7. 65+ CRYSTAL PROFILES TO BUILD OUT
YOUR GRID   159
Before We Begin   159

8. CHOOSING THE RIGHT CRYSTAL FOR
THE JOB   249
Spiritual Enhancement   249
Prosperity and Abundance   250
Emotional Healing   251
Physical Healing   252
Bonus: 6 Intense and Powerful Crystals and
Stones   253
Other Factors to Consider for Crystal
Selection   258

9. PREPARING YOUR CRYSTALS   263
Cleansing and Purifying Crystals   263
Programming Your Crystals   272
Putting It All Together to Get Your Crystals
Ready for the Crystal Grid   273

PART FOUR
SUPERCHARGE YOUR CRYSTALS
THROUGH GRIDWORK

10. 4 SIMPLE STEPS TO CREATE YOUR
    CRYSTAL GRID   277
    How to Build Your Crystal Grid   277
    Maintaining Your Crystal Grid   279
    Crystal Grid Recipes   280
    Additional Tips   291
    Managing Expectations   291

    Conclusion   293
    References   297

"A witch does not need to fix problems. She fixes the energy AROUND problems. Then the problems fix themselves."

— DACHA AVELIN

INTRODUCTION

In the middle of everything she was doing as a housewife, mother, and small-business owner, Nancy often felt lost and alone. She had spent most of her 30s and 40s caring for her family. When her kids finally left home to forge their own paths, leaving an empty nest behind, she didn't know what to do with herself. Her husband had his job, and she had her small business too—but it wasn't enough to make up for the yawning gap left behind by her kids leaving. She tried therapy and several prescription medications, but nothing eased her constant battle with anxiety and grief.

One day, while rummaging the internet for possible ways to heal, she came across a book on witchcraft and holistic healing. Nancy had always been curious, and the topic piqued her interest. She was skeptical, but something about the book's beautiful sparkling crystal cover spoke to her worn soul. She decided to take a chance on the book. After all, she'd tried the conventional solutions, and they hadn't done anything for her. Even if this didn't help, it most certainly wouldn't hurt.

What she didn't expect was that her life would change forever. She spent hours getting lost in the world of crystals and related witchcraft. Until this point, she had thought this was something pagan, only done as a means of escape. Now, however, she saw that witchcraft was not an escape but a means, a bridge to connect her soul with the rest of her body. It was a way to come into herself and realize she was capable and deserving of living a happy, wholesome life.

With time, Nancy began hosting weekly crystal meditation sessions in her living room. She expanded her small business focused on polymer jewelry and included handmade crystal ornaments and raw crystals to imbue and facilitate healing. She became the light of a small community of women who realized that the simple truth to not feeling lost or alone was to turn inward and embrace witchcraft as a facilitator for healing. Through their collective journeys, these women learned that true healing is internal and that there is no *right* or *singular* way to find it.

They had found what was right *for them*, and today, at the very beginning of this book, I'm here to tell you that you are about to do the same.

From Angelina Jolie and Drew Barrymore to Katy Perry and Madonna, many Hollywood A-listers are increasingly turning to crystals to keep their inner energies intact. There has to be a substantial reason why people with access to all the healthcare facilities in the world *voluntarily* choose to walk the route of crystal healing. If you ask me, it's because of the intrinsic energy within crystals. Once you learn to harness this energy and all the well-known (and not-so-well-known) ways to make it work for you, you'll find that life becomes the very thing it's meant to be—easy, nourishing, enjoyable, and, most of all, *fulfilling.*

Dear reader, if you're on this page today, you've come here with an established interest in harnessing the power of crystals through witchcraft. You may be at a crossroads in your life. There was a time when I, much like many of you, felt disillusioned with the world. I had all the apparent comforts—a happy home, good children, and a husband who took care of his own. But even with all of it, I felt tired all the time. It was as if I jumped from one task to the next, with never enough time to connect with myself or the Earth around me. Whenever I tried to voice my concerns, I was ridiculed for believing in superstition and nonsense.

In truth, what I wanted was simple. I desired a meaningful connection to the world around me and to live a purposeful life. The more I delved into it, the more I found that the biggest reason for my unhappiness was how incomplete I felt. There was a vessel of hurt within, from years of pent-up feelings, conflicts I had buried under the carpet, and tiny issues that had bubbled and risen to the surface. And unless I found a way to process and let go of what had broken me, I'd never be able to enjoy life fully.

When I stumbled into the world of witchcraft, I first intended to see if it could help me come to terms with what I had become. At the time, I was like a machine going through the motions of routine life. Witchcraft gave me much more than what I'd expected. I knew I wanted a way to harness the natural world's powers to heal myself and others, but I wasn't sure where to begin. I needed a guide that could make me feel heard and valued and help me connect with the larger purpose of life. And that was what witchcraft did.

Witchcraft originated from *Paganism*, a spiritual practice of loving and revering the Earth. Isn't that so beautiful? The Earth is where we all come from. It makes us whole and what we call home, so in essence, witchcraft *is* the way for all to become attuned to the roots of our existence. The term "witch" has become very nuanced in the contemporary age. People who practice magic have different names. But overall, we all impact the planet in big and small ways.

In the contemporary context, witchcraft has also evolved and expanded as a term. Today, you can be a witch for purely secular reasons. Your love and dedication to the craft may have nothing to do with religion. To me, a witch is someone deeply connected with themselves and the larger universe of energies, including plants, animals, and people. They know how to work with their intrinsic powers to bring about change in the world around them.

In the Romantic age, poets wrote love letters to nature, appreciating her profound beauty. Today, some witches might do the same by caring for and worshiping the natural world and its connected components. From embracing petrichor in the wake of a rainstorm to balancing ourselves in the context of the larger world, we are on track to not just surviving but *living* in the 21st century. My age-old love of witchcraft began when I focused on spending time in nature with my crystals, soaking up sliver fractions of pale sunlight and recon-necting with the rich soil under my feet.

In time, I could sense the deep-seated power thrumming around and beneath me, connecting to the energies I manifested through my crystals and pouring into the vessel of learning and love that I had become.

I breathed deeply and smiled when I saw a little grass flower or heard an owl's hoot. I let my crystals show me the way. And in time, I understood that mental health was never meant to be complicated. We were the ones adding all the unnecessary frills, from the pills and syrups to the hours spent thinking we'd never be good enough. And then, the spring season began in my life. The shadows of dark anxiety no longer trapped me. Instead, a feeling of slender and soft hope crept in, telling me this was my calling and healing.

If you're like me, you want to connect with something bigger than yourself. You want a way to heal that is rooted in nature, a way out of the intense emotional and physical discomfort that has become as routine as waking up and going to bed. You also see your loved ones suffering the same modern-day afflictions and want to help them. And you've come to the right place!

Today, after spending decades being a student of the natural world, I'm here to spill some of the most life-changing secrets on vital gemstones and crystals and tell you ways they can heal you *for good*. You may be here after reading my first book—*Crystal Witchcraft for Beginners*, or you may be new to this world. In either case, you're in the right place.

As a healer and a witch, every single one of you is deeply connected to me. By helping you delve deep and uncover the truth of existence, I hope to share my gift and leave an impact that touches your life like the gentle warmth of yellow, soothing sunshine.

Together, we will further our knowledge about crystals and their powers. You will learn how to use them as component tools in witchcraft to get closure and embrace every second of this precious life!

And one day, you may be sitting where I am, out in an open field under a rustling cicada, writing the introduction to what you hope will heal the world around you a little more because that is the beauty of what we do. When we heal, we do it for ourselves, but we also uplift and rejuvenate the world by extension.

Have you seen how uplifting it feels to be around someone with positive inner energy? It touches you and improves your mood, even if they do nothing but talk, laugh, or share stories. Positive and negative energies are infectious, and for those of you who seek the light, you may benefit the world by simply being yourself.

By the end of this book, I hope to see you in a place where you become the guardian and keeper of secrets to the best kind of existence—*a happy one.*

And yes, while you can employ what you learn to help others, remember that this is entirely based on individual preferences. You are obligated to no one but your own inner energy. So as long as you are keeping that healthy and vital, you're good. As they say, *charity begins at home.* Embrace witchcraft as a means to help yourself first, and then, only if and when you are ready, extend it to the external world.

So, where are we going with this book? I'd say lots of places! From delving into crystal profiles and learning about the essential ones you need in your crystal collection to uncovering crystal grid recipes and spells for prosperity, love, and healing, we will do it all.

You will be equipped with everything you need to enhance your innate internal powers and energies by using crystal grids. In essence, you will enhance your witchcraft practice to make your body a better home for your soul.

Are you ready to begin? Come on, then!

You have been hurting for far too long.

Now, it is time to heal.

PART ONE
THE WONDERS OF CRYSTAL MAGIC AND CRYSTAL GRIDS

CHAPTER 1

A GLIMPSE INTO CRYSTAL MAGIC

This chapter will explore the use of crystals throughout history. We aim to prepare you for what's coming later in the book because the best way to begin a topic is with a little perspective. If you're interested in a more detailed guide to the background of crystals, my first book will get you there!

CRYSTALS THROUGHOUT HISTORY

Crystals have been utilized for their healing properties for centuries. Various traditions and cultures have developed their own unique systems of manifesting these fascinating, beautiful gems to promote emotional, spiritual, and physical well-being. The history of crystals for healing is a diverse, rich tapestry of practices, beliefs, and traditions spanning different civilizations. Over the next few sections, we will delve deeper into the origins, evolution, and enduring appeal of crystal healing.

Ancient Sumerians

The Sumerians lived in Mesopotamia between 4500 and 1900 BCE. They are credited as the first civilization to harness crystals for healing. This ancient populace believed crystals bore a special connection to the divine and could be used to establish communication with the Gods, heal the sick, and offer all kinds of protection against evils.

The Sumerians used various crystals for their healing properties, including quartz, lapis lazuli, and carnelian. Lapis lazuli was idolized for its deep blue color. It was thought to have mystical properties and was used in statues, jewelry, amulets, and even ground into a blue-pigmented powder that was featured in beautiful Sumerian art. The Sumerians also referenced crystals in their mythological depictions. For instance, the goddess of love, Inanna, was depicted venturing to the underworld with a rod and a lapis lazuli necklace for protection (Davis, 2021a). This crystal was said to be one of the deities, and the Sumerians believed it would bring joy and light to whoever embraced it, whether in jewelry or simply by way of practice.

The Sumerians also used crystals during burying rituals. They buried their princess Puabi with gemstones covering her upper body in the form of beads. This would safeguard her soul and invite positive energies to keep the darkness from getting to her. The stones used in her burial included lapis lazuli and carnelian.

Sumerian mythology also speaks of a powerful god, Enki, who had a temple in Eridu. This temple was said to be constructed from lapis lazuli, with its walls adorned with precious stones and gold. Enki was the God of wisdom, magic, and water. His temple was a place of transformational healing, and he could cure any illness. The Sumerians believed his priests used crystals and other sacred tools in their healing practices.

Crystals were also beloved by this civilization for their protective properties. Sumerian amulets of carnelian were worn to safeguard against evil spirits. Quartz was used as a powerful talisman for those going into battle.

The Sumerian civilization pioneered the art of harnessing crystals for protection and healing, laying the groundwork for the many cultures that followed suit. Their belief in the mystical powers of crystals reflected a deep reverence and love for nature in all her glory and a belief that the divine would always exist as a benevolent, preservative force.

Ancient Egyptians

The adoption of crystals in Ancient Egypt can be traced back to the Early Dynastic era (about 3150–c. 2613 BCE) and persisted through the Old Kingdom (around 2613–

2181 BCE), the Middle Kingdom (around 2055–1650 BCE), the New Kingdom (around 1550–1070 BCE), and other dynasties.

Amethyst, carnelian, quartz, and lapis lazuli were only a few of the many crystals used by the Egyptians. Necklaces, bracelets, and earrings made of crystal were popular, as were amulets and talismans made from crystals and worn for protection or health.

Crystals were also utilized in religious rites due to their perceived divine connection. The Eye of Horus, a renowned emblem in Ancient Egyptian mythology, was commonly depicted in lapis lazuli or other blue stones. Crystals were employed for their spiritual and therapeutic abilities and as symbols of riches and power due to their rarity and beauty (Gemporia, 2018). For instance, the Pharaohs' thrones, crowns, and other regalia were often adorned with priceless stones and crystals.

Ancient Egyptians also used crystals in rituals involving the burying of the dead. It was widely held that the energies contained within these precious gems would help guide the dead in the afterlife.

One of the most popular crystals in Ancient Egypt was the lapis lazuli. It was held that the Egyptian queen Cleopatra (69–30 BC) used it in powdered form to adorn her eyes, as we do with eye shadow today. Perhaps the most famous use for lapis lazuli would be the death mask made for Tutankhamun (King Tut). The stone was also found in jewelry pieces uncovered in his tomb, along with carnelian, turquoise, and other precious gems.

Lapis lazuli was so loved and prized by ancient Egyptians that they placed it on a god-like pedestal. The dead kings of ancient Egypt were believed to be revived to consciousness by the sun god *Ra,* who was said to have bones of silver, flesh of gold, and lapis lazuli hair. This crystal has golden specks on a base that is as blue as the Pacific, so many have compared it to the deep quiet of the night sky. To the ancient Egyptians, it symbolized life—including gods and the heavens. Lapis lazuli featured in sacred amulets all across ancient Egypt. It was often molded into a scarab beetle depicting resurrection, renewal, and protection.

The ancient Egyptians were truly captivated by the breathtaking beauty of lapis lazuli. They held this gemstone in high regard and used it extensively, from jewelry to amulets to adorn the walls of their most revered monuments. However, the local supply was not enough to meet the demand of the Egyptians, and they found themselves seeking this precious stone elsewhere.

In their quest to locate more, the ancient Egyptians ventured beyond their borders and sought out nations they could conquer and trade routes they could exploit. One of the most significant sources of lapis lazuli for the ancient Egyptians was the Sar-i Sang mine located in the Badakhshan region of Afghanistan. This mine has been in operation for over 7,000 years and continues to produce high-quality lapis lazuli, which remains in high demand today.

The Sar-i Sang mine was the source of the magnificent lapis lazuli pieces that adorned the burial mask of Tutankhamun, the famous pharaoh boy of Egypt. The mask was crafted using solid gold and inlaid with various precious stones, including lapis lazuli used for the eyebrows, the stripes on the headdress, and the broad collar. In fact, the mask is one of the most impressive and well-known examples of lapis lazuli's use in ancient Egypt. This stunning gemstone was also used to decorate the walls of tombs and temples and ground down into a fine powder to make the vibrant blue pigment used in Egyptian art.

Today, lapis lazuli remains a highly sought-after gemstone, prized for its beauty and rarity. Its rich blue hue and fascinating history make it a gemstone like no other, a true testament to the lasting legacy of the ancient Egyptians and their love for this precious stone. Another famous crystal beloved by ancient Egyptians was turquoise, mined since at least 6000 BC. What is astonishing is that the mines Egyptians sourced turquoise from continue to operate even today!

Located in the Sinai Peninsula, they produced precious gems that went on to adorn the necks of powerful ancient pharaohs. Egyptian turquoise is prized for its beautifully rare translucent, azure color. In 1914, the British School of Archaeology (BSAE) excavated the tomb of

Sithathoryunet, who was possibly a king's daughter. Among the pieces found in her tomb was a magnificent necklace featuring lapis lazuli, gold, carnelian, garnet, feldspar, and turquoise.

In addition to lapis lazuli and turquoise, the ancient Egyptians utilized many other stones in their jewelry and medicinal practices. These stones included amethyst, chalcedony, feldspar, garnet, jasper, obsidian, olivine, and quartz. Ancient Egyptians valued the green-hued malachite, although it was not used in their jewelry. Instead, malachite was powdered down and used as eye makeup.

Many other stones were also used during this era, including green jasper. This particular stone was found in a gold ring that dates back to around 332 BC, which many historians consider the end of this period. The ring features an intricately carved image of Ptah, the God of architecture and craftsmanship. This ring is prominently displayed on this article's opening spread, showcasing the ancient Egyptians' remarkable craftsmanship and use of various stones in their artwork.

Ancient Chinese

The use of crystals for their therapeutic benefits has a long and storied history in China. Crystals have been employed in several medicinal practices, from feng shui to energy balancing, for over 5,000 years.

The ancient Chinese discipline of *feng shui* emphasizes the strategic placement of furniture and other physical elements to maximize the flow of beneficial *chi* (energy). Crystals may be carefully placed throughout a house or workplace to boost positive energy flow and create a sense of harmony (Gemporia, 2018).

Crystals were vital in traditional Chinese medicine since they were utilized to realign the body and restore health. The use of crystals for healing in China is deeply rooted in understanding the balance between elements. The Chinese held that every human being was the sum of different elements—earth, wood, fire, metal, and water and that this pentad required harmony in order to thrive.

Different minerals and elements provide their own distinct vibrational frequencies to crystals. These sound waves have the potential to harmonize and heal by influencing the body's energy fields.

Piezoelectricity, the ability to produce an electric charge in response to mechanical stress, is a unique property of crystals. This charge can facilitate healing at the cellular level. It was thought that the crystals' unique qualities might mend discord and improve people's health and well-being in general.

Jade is one of the most well-known examples of a Chinese crystal. Since ancient times, people have revered jade for its reputed healing abilities and as a representation of virtuous beauty. Ancient cultures believed that jade could restore harmony to the body's energy system, boost the immune system, and extend life expectancy.

The ancient Chinese greatly valued various crystals. While lapis lazuli was worn to increase knowledge and mental clarity, citrine was supposed to bring financial success. Quartz crystals are commonly used to aid concentration, while amethysts are said to heighten psychic abilities.

Ancient Greeks and Romans

Greece was not widely known as an origin point for gemstones, but they existed and abounded there, too. There were rubies from Xanthi, beryl and sapphire from Naxos Island, red garnets (spessartine) from Parson Island, green prase quartz from Serifos, and smithsonite from the Lavrion mines. The Greeks began importing precious gems and stones through the Silk Road in 1600 BC. They sourced these stones from the Far East, Sri Lanka, and India. These were then used to make jewelry. By 300 BC, they also began using semi-precious gemstones.

Greek jewelry drew inspiration from different cultures all over the world. They inlaid their adornments with emeralds, garnet, agate, peridot, carnelian, and rock crystals. In their mythology, Theia, one of the 12 Titans and the daughter of the goddess of Earth (Gaia) and the God of the sky (Uranus), was the one who bestowed shining brilliance on silver, gold, and gemstones. She is revered as the goddess of gems.

Jewelry in ancient Greece was more than decoration. It was a symbol of social status and power. It also worked to attract love and ward off evil, signifying a way to celebrate gods. Even today, Greek jewelry is inlaid with semi-precious stones and gemstones.

In ancient Greece, the dead were buried with their personal treasures. The Greeks believed these would be necessary for the afterlife and that life did not end with death. In fact, they held the belief that there was no death, merely a transition from one state of existence to another. Among other stones, star sapphires were especially coveted among the Greeks because when the stone moved or the light upon its surface changed, it was as if a guiding star came into vision. This was thought to protect owners from envy and harm. It is no coincidence that even today, the amulets for warding off the evil eye are made of beautiful blue sapphires!

Many first-class citizens in ancient Rome wore amulets and protective talismans composed of crystal. These were usually worn to display status or wealth but were also meant to attract good health, prosperity, and favorable outcomes in battle. Rose quartz, for instance, was used by ancient Romans as a way to certify ownership and status. *Intaglios* were carved gemstones mounted in rings. They were popular in Rome for both their aesthetic and practical uses.

The earliest intaglios were made with soft stones that were easy to carve. By the Roman Imperial period, both precious and semi-precious gemstones became the preferred medium for making these ring mounts. Popular choices for intaglios included amethyst, carnelian, and garnet. These were favored for their brilliant colors and translucence. Lapis lazuli and onyx were also deemed valuable for their quality and bold colors.

Native Americans

Ancient Native American cultures used crystals in various ways for both healing and spiritual practices. The Innu tribe, for instance, revered labradorite as a firestone because of its beauty, radiance, and how it seemed to reflect and mirror the Northern Lights. It was widely believed that labradorite had magical properties.

In Native American culture, a legend exists that an Inuit warrior discovered a stunning array of colors inside a labradorite stone and thought these were aurora lights trapped inside the rocks. He whacked them with his spear to free them to the skies. The light that remained on Earth did so in the form of labradorite gemstones (Davis, 2021b). Another story attributed to the Native American Innu people tells the story of stars living beyond the aurora. It was said that they once resided on Earth within labradorite gemstones.

Within Native American cultures, crystals were deeply respected for their unique energies, and it was believed their powers could be harnessed to generate balance, healing, and harmony in both the human body and mind. A common practice was to use crystals in talismans and amulets. These were worn as a form of protection and also to enhance well-being.

Amulets were often carved from crystals like jade, quartz, and turquoise. They were meant to ward off negative energy and attract positive energy. Besides this, crystals also played a prominent role in healing rituals and ceremonies, where healers would place them on or near the body of the one seeking healing. The crystal would then balance the energies in the individual and promote healing in the affected region. Different crystals were thought to have various properties. Healers would select a crystal based on the kind of ailment or condition they needed to heal.

Crystals were also a part of vision quests and other spiritual practices that were believed to help people connect with themselves and the divine. In many cases, healers also used them to improve and establish communal peace. Whenever someone within a community would fall sick, the tightly knit social structure would face turmoil.

Healers would then use gemstones, symbols, and sacred herbs like palo santo and sage to officiate ceremonies for eliminating lingering negative energies. This would revitalize the community and restore its balance.

Crystal healing within Native American cultures was not without a period of upheaval. It is disappointing to think about how often colonizers and explorers attacked societies with deep relationships with stones for their healing potential, dismissing their practices as barbaric and uneducated. Many indigenous communities faced threats to their traditional medicine practices, including using crystals, due to the *Code of Indian Offenses* in the late 19th century.

This code banned the use of healing devices, and those who violated it faced imprisonment or worse. The code remained in effect for almost 50 years, until 1978 when the United States Federal Government, under President Jimmy Carter, acknowledged and reversed the abuse of religious and spiritual practices of indigenous peoples by enshrining their protection in the American Indian Religious Freedom Act.

Today, the treatment methods and practices central to indigenous life for centuries are recognized as complementary and alternative medicines essential for a holistic approach to health and well-being. The history of crystals used in healing throughout Native American tribes is deeply layered and nuanced. It boasts a rich heritage spanning over 2,000 distinct tribes spread across North America alone. The most revered gemstones in Native American cultures included lapis lazuli, black onyx, tiger's eye, amber, agate, jasper, carnelian, and labradorite.

It is human nature to seek out things that will help us elevate ourselves. And that is beautiful because it speaks of our resilience as a species. Perhaps that is why we are so intrinsically drawn to crystals and their uplifting energies.

RELIGIOUS PRACTICES AND CRYSTALS

Now that we have brushed up briefly on the history of crystals used in different ancient cultures, let us take some time to look at how various religions have embraced them as a form of healing and rejuvenation.

Crystals in Christianity

In Christianity, it is believed that crystals, like us human beings, were created by God. The Bible stated that parts of God's heavenly city, New Jerusalem, would be furnished entirely from crystal (Bibleinfo, n.d.). Revelation 21:11, & 18-20 NIV stated that the crystals would shine, and the city would shine with the glory of God—its brilliance comparable to a precious jewel, akin to a jasper and clear like a crystal. The walls of this city would be built with jasper, and the city itself would be of pure gold, pure like glass.

Every manner of precious stone would hold the foundations. The first would be jasper, and the second would be sapphire. The third foundation would comprise chalcedony, the fourth emerald, and the fifth would be made of sardonyx. The sixth foundation would rise from carnelian, the seventh chrysolite. Beryl would uphold the eighth foundation, while topaz would be the heart of the ninth. The tenth would be chrysoprase, the eleventh would be jacinth, and the final would be amethyst.

The Hebrews sourced gemstones from India, Egypt, and the Middle East. During the Exodus, the Bible says that the Israelites carried gemstones with them. This is written in the Book of Exodus, iii, 22; xii, 35-36. When settling in the Land of Israel, the Israelites obtained gemstones via merchant caravans that traveled from Persia and Babylonia to Egypt. They also sourced them from merchants who traveled to Tyre from Saba and Raamah. King Solomon famously equipped a fleet returning from Ophir, which was laden with a manner of precious gems.

The breastplate of the High Priest of Israel, as chronicled in the Book of Exodus, xxvii, 17-20; xxix, 10-13, was said to be adorned with gemstones. The twelve stones of the breastplate and two of the shoulder ornaments were deemed precious by the Jews. Gemstones are also mentioned in the treasure of the King of Tyre in the Book of Ezekiel, xxviii, 13. When the Septuagint translation was done, the specific stones referred to by Hebrew names were no longer recognizable, leading translators to use various Greek words instead. Josephus claimed to have seen the actual stones. In ancient times, gemstones were not categorized based on their composition or crystalline structure. Instead, they were named according to their color, use, or country of origin. As a result, stones of similar or identical colors but with different compositions or structures were given the same names.

Additionally, the problem of changing nomenclature existed as names for certain stones evolved. For instance, what was once known as chrysolite is now called topaz, and what was once sapphire is now lazuli. Nonetheless, we do know that many of these stones were highly valued in ancient Egypt, Assyria, and Babylonia.

Crystals in Islam

Precious stones like pearls, coral, and rubies are mentioned in the Qur'an. Both the Sunni and Shia sects have narrations pointing to the Prophet(s), his companions, and Ali wearing rings. The religion has a deep-rooted connection with crystals, particularly through the story of Ali, the fourth caliph of Islam, and his association with four special stones.

According to Islamic tradition, Ali possessed four stones believed to bring him immense power and wisdom. Each stone was said to have unique properties and qualities that Ali and his followers highly valued. Tradition also states that he wore four rings on his hand. One was opal (yaqut) for dignity and beauty. The other was turquoise (feruz) for divine help. Then there was iron (hadid) for strength, and finally, carnelian (aqiq) for protection from any dangers (Pathak, 2015).

In addition to the stones associated with Ali, some Islamic scholars believe that crystals uniquely amplify and transmit energy, which can be harnessed for healing and spiritual purposes. Islam has a rich history of using crystals as they are believed to help align the chakras and balance the body's energy, improving physical, emotional, and spiritual well-being.

In Islam, as in many other spiritual traditions, the use of crystals is not just about the physical properties of the stones but also about their spiritual and symbolic meaning. They are seen as a way to connect with the higher power of the universe. There is a reason that followers of the religion wear rings of different stones to enhance piety, endurance, and faith. Stones like feruz and aqiq are recommended to be worn at all times, particularly during prayer.

Perhaps one of the most profound ways to understand the importance of this kind of spirituality within Islam is by looking at the significance of the Black Stone. The Black Stone (Al-Hajar Al-Aswad) is a deeply meaningful rock found in the Kaaba, the holiest Islamic site in Mecca, Saudi Arabia. The stone is roughly 11.81 inches in diameter and is composed of volcanic basalt. Legend has it that this sacred stone directly descended from heaven to Prophet Ibrahim (Abraham) and his son Ismail (Ishmael) as a symbol of God's covenant with humanity.

The Black Stone is significant in Islam and is a vital part of the Hajj pilgrimage to Mecca. The stone is said to have the ability to absolve sins and grant wishes, and touching or kissing it during the Hajj is seen as a way to gain the blessings of Allah.

Pilgrims performing the Hajj walk around the Kaaba seven times counterclockwise, and on the first three circuits, they touch or kiss the Black Stone.

The Black Stone has a rich history and has been the subject of numerous legends and traditions in Islamic lore. Some traditions hold that the stone was originally white but turned black due to the sins of humanity. Others claim that it was broken into pieces during an attack on Mecca but was later restored and set back into the Kaaba.

Crystals in Buddhism

There are varied references to crystals in Buddhist texts, mantras, and manuscripts. One of the widely known ones is *Om mani padme hum*, which means, "The jewel is within the lotus." The jewel is regarded as the one that can fulfill the wish for enlightenment, which is the ultimate goal of all Buddhists. The Dalai Lama breaks it down by saying that the first word, *Om*, refers to the impurities present in the practitioner's mind, body, and speech. It also symbolizes the true nature of a Buddha, that is, someone with an elevated state of existence in these three planes. The path one has to follow to get here is indicated by the next four syllables. *Mani* stands for jewels, signifying the method that will lead to the realization of becoming an enlightened being who lives on love and compassion (BlackTreeLab, 2023).

Padme means lotus, and this symbolizes wisdom. Purity can be achieved by unifying wisdom with a sound method, which is signified by *hum*, indicating indivisibility. The phrase can be taken to mean that the human body, the precious gemstone, and intrinsic wisdom are inseparable from one another.

Crystals also play a role in many Buddhist beliefs. One such belief is that *Vajravarahi*, the queen of heaven, is a diamond sow. Buddhists also refer to the diamond *Dorje*, a sacred rod used to symbolize supreme justice and power. The Dorje stood for acting with compassion and represented wisdom. It was said to suppress evil passions and desires, and it had a powerful healing ability to cleanse the human spirit and body and enhance the influence of other potent stones.

In Chinese Buddhism, the diamond throne, which is the center of all things, was carved from a single diamond and is now said to be buried within the Earth.

Other gemstones have also been referenced. The Buddha's tears, for instance, were said to be rubies. It was also believed that the Chinese paid homage to the Buddha with rubies. Tibetans believed rubies could help counter problems related to producing sperm. Another precious gemstone mentioned in Buddhism is sapphire. This stone is said to be the key to tranquility, serenity, happiness, devotion, and spiritual enlightenment.

Another prominent stone used in Buddhism was turquoise. A Buddhist belief surrounding this stone is that the Buddha once vanquished a monster using a magic turquoise stone. This stone is beloved by Tibetan shamans. They believe it has protective and spiritual properties. It features in shamanic ceremonies, and in China and Tibet, it is also worn as a display of wealth and for protection.

Jade is also prominently used in Buddhist spiritual practices. It represents the four cardinal virtues that are the cornerstones of Buddhism. These are courage, justice, modesty, and purity. Jade was sacred to the Buddha and to the Buddhist goddess Kwan Yin. The Buddhists also hold lapis lazuli in high regard and believe it is one of the eight sacred symbols that signify good luck.

Rose quartz has also been used in many spiritual capacities. It is associated with the Goddess Kwan Yin, who symbolizes compassion, mercy, and peace. The early Chinese used the stone for carvings of the goddess to reflect her wisdom and gentleness through the color of rose quartz. Another stone, amethyst, is also used by Tibetan monks in meditation *malas*. The Tibetans believe this stone is sacred and make prayer beads from it.

Other gemstones used by the Buddhists include green aventurine, carnelian, and chalcedony. Carnelian symbolizes peace and joy and is used to banish sorrow and herald in the good times. Chalcedony's purity is often likened to that of the lotus flower, which is considered holy. Green aventurine is prominently used to carve the eyes of

Tibetan statues because it is said to come with visionary powers.

Tibetan Buddhists used quartz to understand the origins of illnesses. Clear quartz would help understand origins and was also used for diagnostic healing. The Tibetan monks have always held it to be a sacred object of immense power. In Tibetan Buddhism, quartz is also used to fashion prayer beads and to achieve stillness of mind, which is the predominant goal of meditation in Buddhism. In Tibetan Buddhist healing, azurite is said to work as a remedy for kidney diseases, and banded agate also prevents demonic possession.

With that, we conclude our discussion on crystals and their significance in different ancient cultures and religions. Before we move on, let us take some time to delve into the relationship between crystals and witchcraft.

CRYSTALS AND WITCHCRAFT

Wiccan is a term you will hear a lot of in the world of witchcraft. It could be of great or little interest to you, but I'll just pause a second and briefly explain what it is. Wiccan is the largest of the modern pagan religions. Its followers will typically identify as witches. As a Wiccan witch, your source of inspiration would likely come from the pre-Christian religions of Europe. Wiccan followers often use a five-pointed star called the pentagram as the primary religious symbol.

Once again, it helps to remember here that you can practice witchcraft for entirely non-religious reasons. The way I see it, **the urge to heal is human and natural, and it may or may not have anything to do with your religious beliefs.** You could be a witch simply because you want to manifest good energies to help you live a healthy, wholesome life. Or, you could do it for both these reasons and your religious sentiments.

Whatever lane you choose, the intention is always the most important. A Wiccan witch, for example, can use crystals to mark a sacred circle before beginning a ritual. They may also use it for honoring deities. In Wiccan practice, it is also common to use magical tools like pentacles and wands laden with crystals.

When it comes to using crystals in witchcraft, it is important to remember that simply working with them once or twice does not necessarily signify anything deep. As a matter of fact, most witches feel that crystals can work as a means or tool to achieve something, but the result you are looking for will not come simply because you are wielding a crystal. It would help if you also had practice, study, and dedication. You could use a hammer around your house, but that wouldn't automatically make you a construction worker. In the same way, if you use crystals without intention, you'll find that the results you get are, at best, superficial.

Crystal witches are a distinct subset of practitioners with a special connection to the energetic vibrations in gemstones and crystals. They can use them to manifest meaning or amplify natural and magical energies. As a crystal witch, you will have the intrinsic ability to see and feel auras and energies. And just like there are crystal witches, there are also sea, plant, and cosmic witches (among countless others, too). Some of us are also eclectic, which means we like to borrow from different traditions and customize our magical capabilities depending on the circumstances and necessities. Many of us may know how to use some crystals but prefer another way to channel energy. At the end of the day, you can choose to work with crystals because *they speak to you and you want to use them to achieve your purpose.*

Essentially, you become a crystal witch when you are mindfully immersed in understanding crystals and their benefits, and you want to learn to use them for manifesting and healing. Crystals are known to uplift vibrations. This magical thing called crystalline structure means that crystals emit a constant, unwaveringly high vibration. When this meets a low vibration, which could be the energy you are trying to heal, it can raise and heal this lower vibration at an energetic level, propelling a deep state of physical healing.

Crystal witches tend to ailments, conduct spell work, manifestations, and actually— anything they need to stay happy and healthy while using crystals as tools. Note here: the kind of joy you seek cannot be brought forth by the crystal alone. There must be a unison of your mind, intention, *and* the crystal. And when it comes to what crystals you relate to, that is something entirely personal. Go with what your heart chooses and what your energies call your own.

Crystal magic is beautiful because of the interplay of colors involved. These colors vibrate different frequencies of light and resonate with distinct aspects of our lives. Therefore, crystals are unique for different purposes, whether for money matters, health, love, or protection. The color of the rose quartz, for example, is a soft pink. This symbolizes a loving, harmonizing vibration that can be utilized to draw love into our lives. On the other hand, jade is a vibrant green that signifies abundance, making it a good call to bring prosperity.

When it comes to choosing crystals for your practice, you will often hear one phrase: It is widely believed that the crystal chooses you and not the other way around. You could be gifted a stone by a friend or family member or even stumble upon one when hiking a dirt trail. Or, you could purchase a stone from an online shop while setting a clear intention that it is the right one for you.

When you buy a crystal from a shop, you can be drawn to some kinds without needing to think too deeply. You could, for instance, be pulled to a particular type or color. When making your choice, scan your emotional energy and physical body. If you feel positive vibes when you look at and touch the crystal, it may be the one for you. It might not be the right fit if you don't feel anything at all. Crystals, in their purest state, do not give off negative energy. It's just that some may speak more to us than others, so always keep your intuition active.

With that, we come to the end of this chapter. We discussed the role of crystals in ancient cultures, touched upon their importance in different religious practices, and covered aspects of what they could mean in witchcraft. Remember that using a crystal in your witchcraft practice should be because it speaks to you and is something you see yourself doing as a way to live a happier, healthier life.

One of the most intriguing things about using crystals for healing lies within the world of sacred geometry, which ascribes symbolic meanings to distinct geometric shapes and proportions. It will be crucial to your practice, so to learn more about it, let's move on to the next chapter!

CHAPTER 2

THE SECRETS OF THE UNIVERSE AND HOW THEY INFLUENCE CRYSTAL GRIDS

T his chapter will discuss the concept of sacred geometry and delve into its presence as an ancient, omnipresent secret that has made it the building block of the universe. You will learn how to channel its power into grids. From there, we will also do a brief study about the nature of crystal grids and their main components, and it is only brief because we will cover crystal grids in depth in Chapter Ten. Let us begin.

UNDERSTANDING SACRED GEOMETRY

In mathematics, geometry is a branch that explores the existing relationship between different spaces and shapes. You can trace the origins of geometry to 2000 BCE–1001 BCE in Egyptian and Mesopotamian cultures. Over 13 centuries later, at a time when philosophers and thinkers, including Pythagoras, started studying its potentialities, geometry blossomed in ancient Greece. It would, in time, become one of the most exciting and impressive branches of math because it led to the development of various practical principles based on aesthetics and, of course, sacred manifestations.

In formal terms, sacred geometry uses geometric principles in the context of religion. It can be used to define patterns and shapes that have been carved into cathedrals and altars. In a less orthodox and more sensitive way, we can also view these as the patterns existing in the aesthetic beauty of the universe around us. This includes mineral structures, astral formations, and even our genetic code. Geometry is everywhere, both within and around us. Sacred geometry uses art to manifest and reflect the sublime mathematical perfection that exists in nature.

I mentioned that sacred geometry can be traced back to Ancient Egypt. To the early Egyptians, geometry was more than merely studying surfaces, lines, and their properties. They were fascinated by the inherent harmony in geometry and recognized it as the most convincing expression of a divine plan underlying the world. To them, geometry was a metaphysical blueprint that formed the foundation of physical existence.

Ancient Egyptian works are admired because of their proportional harmony. They appeal to our inner and outer aesthetic senses—and this harmonious design shows a core understanding and emulation of the principles of sacred geometry, where all figures can be created with a straight line and a compass, irrespective of rigorous measurements. The key sense here is that of proportion.

Another instance of ancient cultures manifesting the principles of sacred geometry dates back to over 4,500 years ago when Mesopotamian kings wore bracelets engraved with the Flower of Life symbol on them. This symbol is one of the most mystical geometric symbols of all time. It represents the cycle of life and is said to hold the secrets to the creation of the universe within its patterns.

The word *geometry* owes its origins to the Greek words *geo*, meaning "earth," and *metron*, meaning "measurement." The Greeks applied their knowledge of mathematics and geometry to practical tasks, such as surveying and measuring land, and to more abstract pursuits, such as understanding the nature of the universe. They also developed a system of axioms and proofs that formed the foundation of modern geometry. While the Greeks did not invent the term *geometry*, their contributions to the field were so significant that the study of geometry is often associated with ancient Greek culture.

Sacred geometry played a significant role in Greek culture, where it was regarded as a symbol of divine order and harmony. The Greeks believed that the universe was created according to geometric principles and that these principles governed all aspects of life.

The Greeks were particularly fascinated with the golden ratio, a mathematical ratio that abounds in nature and art. The golden ratio is approximately 1.618, often represented by the Greek letter phi. They believed the golden ratio represented beauty, balance, and proportion and incorporated it into their art and architecture.

The golden ratio, for instance, is prominent in Greek architectural marvels like the Parthenon temple in Athens. The Parthenon was built to honor the beloved Greek goddess Athena and is renowned for its harmonious proportions and use of the golden ratio.

The Greeks also believed that certain geometric shapes had spiritual significance. For example, the circle was seen as a symbol of unity and eternity, while the triangle represented the trinity of the gods. The Greeks used these shapes in their art and architecture to convey deeper meanings and to create a sense of harmony and balance.

Various cultures and even entire religions have been influenced by the core concepts of sacred geometry. From ancient times, different cultures have used geometric shapes and patterns to represent their beliefs and connect with the divine.

In Hinduism, the mandala is a sacred symbol for meditation and spiritual reflection. The mandala represents the universe and is often composed of intricate geometric patterns. The lotus flower is another symbol used in Hinduism, and its shape is often incorporated into mandalas to represent spiritual purity and enlightenment.

In Islam, geometric patterns are used extensively in architecture and art. The use of geometry in Islamic art is believed to reflect the Islamic concept of *tawhid,* or the oneness of God. The repetition of geometric patterns is also used to symbolize the infinite nature of God and the universe.

In Christianity, sacred geometry has been used to represent the universe's divine order. The cross is a common symbol in Christianity, and its shape represents the intersection of Heaven and Earth. The rose window, a common feature in Gothic architecture, is often composed of intricate geometric patterns meant to represent the divine light.

The Star of David, a Jewish symbol, represents the connection between God and humanity. The hexagonal shape of the star is believed to reflect the six days of creation and the six directions of the universe.

In many Native American cultures, geometric patterns are used in pottery and textiles to represent spiritual beliefs and traditions. For example, the Navajo rug often incorporates geometric patterns to represent the four cardinal directions and the elements of the natural world.

SACRED GEOMETRY SYMBOLS

There are many beautiful symbols with special meaning in the world of sacred geometry, and one list cannot possibly do justice to all of them. However, in this section, we will go over some of these symbols and explore their origins and meanings.

The Circle

The circle is among the most fundamental geometric shapes and has been an important symbol in sacred geometry across many cultures throughout history. The circle is a beautiful shape that goes on in an infinite loop with no beginning or end, and it represents wholeness, unity, and infinity. It is believed to have originated with ancient Babylonians and Egyptians, who used it to represent the sun and the moon, respectively. In many cultures, the circle is associated with the perpetual cycle of life and death. It is also the base for understanding many cycles of nature, such as the changing seasons (Regan, 2021).

In sacred geometry, the circle represents spiritual unity and the interconnectedness of all things. The circle also symbolizes perfection, as it has no angles or corners and is considered to be the most holistic shape. One interesting story surrounding the importance of the circle in sacred geometry comes from Native American culture. According to the story, a group of young boys went out into the wilderness to fast and pray for a vision that would guide them in their lives. One of the boys envisioned a circle with four points, which he interpreted as representing the four directions and the interconnectedness of all things. This vision became the basis for the medicine wheel, a sacred symbol used by many Native American tribes to represent the balance and harmony of the natural world.

While there are variations in the specifics of the story and its interpretation among different tribes, the core concept of the circle as a symbol of unity and interconnectedness is widely recognized in Native American culture. The medicine wheel is based on balance, harmony, and a sense of togetherness. Nothing exists in isolation; we are all part of something more profound and significant than our individual lives.

The Triangle

The triangle is another important symbol in sacred geometry and has been used across many cultures throughout history. The triangle is a three-sided polygon, and its shape is significant because it is the simplest polygon that cannot be reduced further. In many religions, the triangle symbolizes the trinity or triune nature of divinity in many religions, such as Christianity, Hinduism, and Islam. In sacred geometry, the triangle is associated with stability, strength, and the balance of opposing forces. In Buddhism, the triangle appears as *Trikaya*, the three bodies of essence, enjoyment, and transformation (*Trikaya | Buddhism*, 2019). These represent the bodies of knowledge, Heaven, and Earth, and together, they embody the wholeness of the Buddha. *Abhijna* is one more Buddhist concept symbolized by the triangle. It represents access to knowledge by higher living and thinking, including meditation and concentration.

If you look at books, music album covers, or even artistic decor, you may be surprised at how often the triangle appears. Many generations have been influenced by the divinity behind this one symbol. Artistically, the triangle is evocative of creativity inspired by the harmony existing between opposites. Human creation itself—and by that, I mean the beautiful act of birth—is influenced by feminine and masculine opposites. Similarly, when we look for ways to find answers to a challenge, we counter negative forces with positive ones. Evolution itself is the product of opposing forces propelling us forward.

One interesting story surrounding the importance of the triangle in sacred geometry comes from the ancient Egyptians. According to legend, the God Thoth, the patron of wisdom and knowledge, used the power of the triangle to create the universe. Thoth was believed to have used his knowledge of sacred geometry to form a triangular home to the entire universe's secrets, which was said to be the source of all creation. Another example of the significance of the triangle in sacred geometry comes from Chinese culture, where the triangle is associated with the concept of *qi*, or vital energy. In traditional Chinese medicine and the revered practice of martial arts, this sacred geometry symbol represents the flow of qi throughout the body and the balance of opposing forces.

The Square

The square is one of geometry's most fundamental forms, produced by joining four equal-length lines at right angles. Many cultures have employed this basic form as a sign throughout history, including ancient Egyptian, Chinese, and Greek societies. The square was utilized as a symbol of the Earth and the physical universe in ancient Egypt. It was linked to the goddess Isis, who was revered as the mother goddess and the creator of life. The square is commonly identified with the element of earth and the center of the universe in Chinese culture. It was associated with the deity Apollo and the concepts of balance, harmony, and proportion in ancient Greece.

Numerically, we often link the number four with the shape of a square. This number bears significance in many spiritual traditions. It symbolizes the core elements of fire, water, air, and earth. It also signifies the cardinal directions in different faiths: north, south, east, and west. The square is frequently employed as a graphic depiction of these notions to represent the actual world and material reality.

The spiritual Chinese practice of *feng shui* is closely connected with the square. Going by the principles of feng shui, the design of a structure may significantly influence the flow of energy, or qi. Square-shaped structures are said to be fortunate because they signify balance, stability, and harmony. Buildings with irregular forms or corners, on the other hand, are said to obstruct the flow of energy, causing imbalance and disharmony.

The Cross

The cross is perhaps among the topmost well-known and lasting symbols in human history, with its meaning spread across civilizations and religious traditions. At its most basic, the cross is a simple geometric form composed of two perpendicular lines meeting at a central point. Its importance and meaning, however, extend much beyond its mere design.

The Ankh, utilized as a symbol of perpetual life in ancient Egyptian mythology, is among the first known forms of this symbol. The Ankh, which resembles a cross with a loop at the top, was thought to represent the union of masculine and feminine forces and the omnipresent cycle of life, death, and rebirth. The cross is frequently connected with Jesus Christ's crucifixion in the Christian faith. Per the Bible, Jesus was crucified on the cross. His passing was a reflection of sacrifice for humanity's sins. As a result, the cross became a potent symbol of sacrifice, redemption, and hope, and it is one of Christianity's most important symbols to date.

Many other religious and spiritual traditions throughout history have associated different spiritual meanings with the cross. The swastika, for example, is a Hindu emblem of good luck and wellness, resembling a cross with arms bent at right angles. The cross-legged stance, referred to as the lotus position, is frequently employed during meditation in Buddhism to signify inner balance and harmony. The Celtic tradition has an intriguing narrative concerning the cross. St. Patrick traditionally used the Celtic cross to bring the pagan Irish to Christianity. The Celtic cross blends the Christian cross and a circle, which is said to be representative of the sun, moon, and natural cycles. The circle also represents eternity and the never-ending cycle of existence, demise, and rebirth. As a result, the Celtic cross became a potent emblem of the unity between the spiritual and natural worlds.

A powerful and lasting symbol in sacred geometry with several roots and meanings, whether used to represent Jesus Christ's sacrifice and salvation, the endless cycle of life and death, or the union of spiritual and natural forces, remains a symbol of hope, harmony, and spiritual unification. Its basic geometric design betrays its profound and eternal importance, making it one of human history's most iconic symbols.

The Pentagram

Another symbol that forms the core of sacred geometry is the pentagram. Legend has it that this mysterious symbol dates back to the Mesopotamian civilization that existed over 4,000 years ago. At the time, it could have been used to denote the five planets visible to human eyes. In Ancient Greece, the pentagram was closely tied to the

Goddess Kore, later edified as Persephone. It was symbolic of vitality and health.

You can create the pentagram by drawing a star with five points inside a circle. Each point of this star must touch the circle's edges. It is unique because you can do it with a single, continuous line—you don't even need to lift your pen from the paper. Within the realm of sacred geometry, the pentagram is a powerful representation of balance and protection. The five points mimic a core element. This could be spirit, fire, air, water, or earth. The circle surrounding these points represents all that is divine and infinite. Taken as a whole, the pentagram is said to be a balancing element that can align different forces operating in your body, spirit, and mind and bring them together as one harmonious continuum.

Going back to cultures and religions, in ancient Babylon, the pentagram denoted a symbol to ward off evil spirits. In Hinduism, it was linked to the Goddess Kali, who represents everything fundamental about existence, destruction, and regeneration. In a more contemporary context, the pentagram is linked with different mystical beliefs and often features in core Wiccan and modern witchcraft practices. It depicts the goddess, and when used in spells and rituals, it is said to invoke her divine power.

An interesting account involving the pentagram comes from ancient Greece. Per legend, Pythagoras—a beloved philosopher and mathematician—discovered the pentagram while studying patterns made by Venus as it traversed through the sky. Pythagoras thought the pentagram was a perfect representation of the larger universe and how mystical its forces can be. The pentagram is a fascinating symbol with a rich, deep history and symbolism. Above all, it denotes protection, balance, and the harmony of all existence.

The Sri Yantra

The Sri Yantra is a complex symbol originating in ancient India, and it is one of the most beloved and auspicious symbols that lie at the heart of Hinduism. *Sri Yantra* stands for "sacred instrument." It is a diagrammatic representation of nine interlocking triangles surrounding a *Bindu*, which is a central point. Every triangle represents a different aspect of the divine feminine energy known as *Shakti*. The Bindu is indicative of the divine masculine energy that is called *Shiva*. The Sri Yantra is also called the *Yantra Raja* because of its intricate patterns and the depth of its symbolism. Its origins are shrouded in mystery (Gaia, 2020). Some scholars believe it dates back over 5,000 years to the Vedic times. Yet, others think it was created in medieval India. Regardless of the specifics, it is still widely used in Hinduism today.

A powerful tool for meditation, the Sri Yantra is a visual depiction of the highest level of human consciousness. It helps us achieve our highest selves and rise to levels where we can access and be inspired by the cosmic energies of the universe. The interlocking triangles indicate universal harmony and balance, while the Bindu is the point of origin for all things. According to legend, it is said that there was a group of wise, ancient sages who wanted to build a powerful talisman to safeguard themselves from negative energies and attract good fortune. They consulted with the goddess Devi and learned of the sacred geometry behind the Sri Yantra.

Armed with what they now knew, the sages created a talisman and used it to shield themselves from trouble while filling their lives with abundance. The power of the symbol was so great that it was said to protect them from powerful demons who wanted to destroy them. In contemporary times, the Sri Yantra features in many Hindu ceremonial rituals. It is also employed in meditation, modern spiritual practices, crystal grids, and other forms of energy healing.

The Golden Spiral

A logarithmic spiral, this beautiful shape grows in the same proportions as the venerable golden ratio, a mathematical concept that is upheld for its beauty and harmony. The golden ratio exists in architecture, art, and nature and denotes balance and perfection. In sacred geometry, the spiral symbolizes creation. It is closely tied to the Fibonacci Sequence, which denotes a series of progressively growing numbers. You can see this sequence in flower patterns, the scale of pinecones, and spread across nature. The Fibonacci Sequence was first brought to light by an Italian monk in the 1200s. Both the Golden Spiral and the Fibonacci Sequence are closely connected in sacred geometry. In math, the Fibonacci Sequence denotes a pattern where each number results from the sum of the two numbers before it, beginning with 0 and 1. The pattern goes 0, 1, 1, 2, 3, 5, 8, and so on.

Consequently, the Golden Spiral is said to expand according to the Fibonacci Sequence, which is created by drawing a series of squares whose side lengths correspond to the Fibonacci numbers. The spiral is then created by drawing quarter-circles inside each square, connecting their corners. This results in a spiral that expands according to the Fibonacci Sequence. The Golden Spiral can be seen in many natural phenomena, including the shape of seashells, the spiral arms of galaxies, and the arrangement of leaves on a stem. It also exists in the design of many ancient structures, such as the Parthenon in Greece and the Great Pyramids of Egypt.

The Golden Spiral is believed to represent growth, expansion, and the interconnectedness of all things. It depicts harmony and balance, embodying the natural order of the universe. Think about it yourself. Even when you consider the cycle of fruit trees, you will see the Golden Spiral at play. Each fruit tree produces a flower that is subsequently germinated to turn into a fruit. The fruit has seeds that fall to the ground or are carried to other places by birds and the wind—eventually growing into another tree. This simple addition of things is fundamental to both the way the world functions and the Golden Spiral.

One interesting story surrounding the Golden Spiral comes from the Renaissance artist Leonardo da Vinci. He was fascinated by it and saw it as a representation of divine proportion. He used the spiral in many artworks, including the famous Mona Lisa, which can be seen in how her hair is arranged and in the shape of her body. Da Vinci believed the Golden Spiral was the key to creating perfect beauty in art and architecture.

The Labyrinth

An ancient archetype, labyrinths date back 4,000 years or earlier. In symbolic terms, they can be likened to a choreographed dance, walking meditation, or the site of a ceremony or ritual. They are tools for psychological, spiritual, and personal transformation. They are deeply connected to sacred geometry, metaphors, religious practice, mindfulness, and everything that is spiritual about human nature. Walking or interacting within a labyrinth is said to activate physical responses like increased quiet, calmness, and a state of relaxation. You feel your agitations decrease and are no longer burdened by the weight of stress and anxiety. This is known as the Labyrinth Effect, and it allows you to respond to everything with a clear state of mind, openness, peace, clarity, and solid reflection. You also become more receptive to hearing the words of wisdom of your inner voice and develop solid insight into meaningful intuition that will steer you in the right direction.

Labyrinths are found in numerous places around our world. Regardless of their location, all of them have certain similarities in design. The global fascination surrounding this sacred geometry shape has been volatile but never died out—classical labyrinths date back the farthest, followed by Roman and medieval labyrinths. The essential features include a bounded interior that demarcates the outer region. There is a continuous, meandering path to the core and then back out, mostly by the same path. Labyrinths are often made using stone, tile, grass, soil, carved wood, and even painted canvas.

True labyrinths have a single path (unicursal), unlike multicursal mazes. They exist to give people a spiritual experience. The same path may wind forward and back repeatedly. Some labyrinths have distinctly different features, like the absence of a central space and various intersections. It is still a singular path that can loop, double back, and include miles and miles of walking. But there are no opportunities to lose yourself, only ones for greater internal discovery. In truth, only one path exists, and it leads in and out.

In Greek mythology, the labyrinth was a structure built by the artificer Daedalus for King Minos. It was intended to hold the minotaur, a monster eventually killed by the hero Theseus. It was said to be so elaborate that even Daedalus had trouble getting out of it once he made it. Meditation through the walking of a labyrinth has been practiced for ages. These days, they're often constructed outside, either as discrete hedges or as part of a larger route laid out in stones and paved with soil. They are large enough to create a path for the introspective to follow when meditating, and they are constructed into the flooring of medieval cathedrals.

Walking toward a central point is integral to the practice; while walking, one's gaze is directed downward so that one may concentrate on the ground beneath rather than the sights and sounds around them. When subjected to monotony and a lack of stimulation, the mind naturally looks within and upward. The practitioner's feet eventually cease moving and arrive at the center. This is where the minotaur is thought to live. Perhaps it is the heart of our intrusive thoughts, the ones we must rise above in the journey to reach our highest selves.

The Flower of Life

The exact origins of the Flower of Life symbol are not entirely clear, as it exists across different historical periods and cultures. The oldest known instance is found at the Temple of Osiris in Abydos, Egypt, which is believed to be more than 6,000 years old. This symbol is also etched across ancient Christian churches, Jewish synagogues, and Hindu temples—suggesting its universal nature of existence.

Many scholars believe the Flower of Life to be a visual representation of creation and the underlying unity of everything. There's also the belief that this symbol denotes the very blueprint of our universe and how each component is connected to the next. Geometrically, this symbol is a pattern of 19 circles that overlap and are arranged with meticulous care—forming a larger, over-encompassing circle. The overlapping circles bear a sixfold symmetry and resemble the petals of a flower, resulting in a pattern that can help you enter a deep state of meditation and peace. The name itself dates back to the 1990s when it was first used in *The Ancient Secret of the Flower of Life, Vol. 1* in 1999.

Today, you can see the Flower of Life represented in jewelry because of its inherent symmetry and aesthetics. Its use is most revered in religious structures, including altars, churches, temples, and mosques. The Flower of Life is apparent in many of the Osireion's columns. This was part of the sacred Temple of Seti I in Egypt. The symbol is also used in Phoenician art, going back as far as the ninth century BCE. Famous artists, including Leonardo da Vinci, were mesmerized by the pattern. In his depiction of the *Vitruvian Man*, he is said to have been inspired by his love for the Flower of Life.

Within New Age circles, the Flower of Life's central circle signifies that all life originates from one source. The geometric pattern also denotes enlightenment and spiritual progress. Many religions believe that life is begotten from one supreme, higher power—which ties in with these religions' core beliefs.

Patterns Related to The Flower of Life

The Tree of Life, Circle of Life, Vesica Piscis, Tripod of Life, Seed of Life, Egg of Life, and Fruit of Life are some of the most prominent and recognized symbols in sacred geometry (Nguyen, 2023).

The Tree of Life is prominent in many cultures and religions. It signifies the interconnectivity of all living creatures and the cycles of birth, growth, death, and rebirth. The Tree of Life is frequently represented as a gigantic tree with deep earthen roots and branches reaching the sky. It is thought to represent the union of Heaven and Earth and the balance of masculine and feminine energy. In its simplest form, it is characterized by ten circles that form the shape of a tall standing tower with a narrow base.

Another prominent symbol in sacred geometry is the **Circle of Life**. It also symbolizes life's cyclical cycle and the interconnection of all things. The Circle of Life is sometimes portrayed as a circle including numerous symbols and patterns, such as the Tree of Life, flowers, and other natural components. The **Vesica Piscis** symbol is formed by crossing two identical circles such that their edges meet. It signifies the meeting of the earthly realm with the heavenly one and the harmony of the spiritual and physical realms. Throughout history, the Vesica Piscis has been employed in different types of art and construction, including stained glass windows, mosaics, and paintings.

Three interconnecting circles form the **Tripod of Life**. It symbolizes the three facets of life: physical, mental, and spiritual. In meditation and spiritual practices, the Tripod of Life assists in balancing and harmonizing these three parts of the self. The **Seed of Life** is a seven-circle overlapping emblem. In the Judeo-Christian faith, it stands for the seven days of creation, while in Hinduism and Buddhism, it represents the seven chakras. It is frequently employed in meditation and healing activities to encourage spiritual growth and change.

The **Egg of Life** can sometimes be depicted as a three-dimensional cube represented by seven circles. It can also be depicted as a component within the context of the flower of life, where six additional circles are shown overlapping the original seven-circle shape, creating a geometrically structured design of 13 circles. This symbol is said to represent the universe's 13 stages of formation, from the Big Bang to the present. In spiritual practices, the Egg of Life stimulates creativity, development, and transformation. The **Fruit of Life** comprises 13 circles arranged similarly to a six-sided star. It is thought to contain the origin information of the cosmos and all living things. It is an integral part of many spiritual and meditation activities that work to create balance, harmony, and connection with the cosmos.

Sacred geometry symbols represent some of the most significant and powerful parts of the human experience. These symbols give a framework for comprehending the surrounding universe and our related positions, from the connectivity of all living things to the cyclical rhythm of life and the balance between the spiritual and physical worlds. The Tree of Life, Circle of Life, Vesica Piscis, Tripod of Life, Seed of Life, Egg of Life, and Fruit of Life —whether employed in meditation, healing, or creative activities—provide a robust and meaningful method to connect with the cosmos and encourage spiritual growth and transformation.

Metatron's Cube

Named after the archangel Metatron, this sacred geometry shape is a two-dimensional form that occurs by interconnecting all the circles from what is also known as its sister symbol, a.k.a. the Fruit of Life. The Fruit of Life is almost identical to Metatron's Cube, but it does not have lines, only circles. In 3D form, this shape resembles a Merkaba formed by the intersection of two pyramids. The Metatron's Cube explains and signifies the birth of the universe and its natural way of existence by infinitely reaching through all dimensions of space and time. Much like other origin theories, this symbol also begins from a singular point and reaches outward.

Everything in this universe, including the very galaxies, solar systems, stars, various planets, component living creatures and their DNA structures, electrons, and even nanoparticles, rise from the same fundamental elements, and they all follow the very same basic mathematical laws of physics and nature. The laws and principles that underlie the functioning and interaction of and between these elements are thought to be written in the composition of Metatron's Cube.

The cube's exact origins are unclear, but it could date back to ancient Jewish mysticism, particularly the Kabbalah tradition. Kabbalah is a subsect of Jewish mysticism that surrounds the nature of the universe and the divine by symbolically interpreting the Hebrew Bible and other religious documents. It is a Merkaba cube representing the crown on the Tree of Life and, therefore, a symbol of complete compassion. The Metatron's Cube is thought to contain five key sacred shapes that are at the heart of all matter in existence.

These are known as the platonic solids, also called the perfect solids, because every face of each of these symbols bears an equal side length, face size, and angle. They also fit perfectly in a sphere. These solids were named after Plato, who was influenced by Pythagoras. To them, the secret key to unlock the base of all matter is Metatron's Cube. In itself, the Metatron's Cube is a reminder that the universe favors us when we unearth our personal powers, using them to do good to ourselves and the world around us. In New Age spirituality, it is a visualization and manifestation tool that can help align our human energies with the divine.

SUMMING UP

Witchcraft, to me, is deeply symbolic and intuitive. It helps us connect with the natural world and what we perceive as divine, allowing us to channel the positive energies around us and within ourselves to heal and thrive. Sacred geometry, the study of shapes and patterns that inherently occur in nature and the world around us, is a fundamental part of who you aim to become. As a witch, open yourself up to all the cues from the natural environment surrounding you. A great way to do this is to have a sketchbook or notepad with you at all times. You never know when inspiration or vision could strike! Whenever you encounter a shape or symbol that speaks to you—and believe me, you will because this is inherent in us all—write it down or make a rough sketch of it.

It could be anything from a twirling leaf to a building pattern to the shape of a coffee cup. The fact that you spotted a symbol is a sign that the universe wants you to get inspired. Another great way to harness the powers of sacred geometry is by visiting locations in real time. When opportunities come your way, go to places that are rich in symbolism and history. You may chance upon ancient ruins, stone circles, and other excavation sites that abound in patterns and symbols that can truly help your practice and even inspire you to design your own patterns.

On that note, don't shy away from letting your artistic and creative self shine! Creating your own shapes is a powerful way to connect with and lean into the moreish nature of sacred geometry and allow it to become a natural part of your life. These shapes could simply have a special meaning to you, and you can use them in your spells, gridwork, and other areas of your personal life. Whether it signifies an intention or speaks to your soul, a self-created symbol is an excellent way to reach within and channel your inner spiritual powers. Incorporating sacred geometry into your practices will help you form deeper connections. An important thing to remember is to always be curious and open to the signs of the universe. You will find that once you open yourself up to them, they will show up for you again and again.

Understanding the significance and purpose behind each form and pattern in sacred geometry is essential in your spells and rituals. For instance, the Tree of Life depicts expansion and the link between material and spiritual realms, while the Circle of Life reflects the interdependence of all things. Once you learn the meaning of these symbols, you may include them in your rituals and spells to increase their efficacy. Among sacred geometry's many potent symbols is the Tripod of Life. It symbolizes the divine in its three guises: creator, preserver, and destroyer. You may use this symbol in rituals and spells to bring harmony to these three components of your being.

Using sacred geometry in your rituals and spells is a great way to deepen their significance and enrich your spiritual experience. To make a divine connection, all you need to do is be receptive to the symbols and forms in your environment. There is no one correct method for engaging in intuitive and symbolic witchcraft. The options are vast, whether you want to use conventional symbols or make your own. It's a distinctive path nobody else can take except you. Embrace what speaks to you, and never hesitate to try new things.

In summary, sacred geometry has been employed for generations to gain insight into the cosmos and establish a rapport with the divine. You may benefit from its ancient knowledge and advance on your spiritual path by integrating it into your practice. You are a student of everything in the universe, including yourself, nature, and life. Be receptive to the signs and omens surrounding you and use them to inform and direct your actions.

CRYSTAL GRIDS

So, we learned all about the mystical power attached to shapes and symbols. This brings us to the topic of crystal grids, which, in plain speak, is the art of intentionally arranging several crystals in different patterns and shapes. It's extraordinary how doing something like this can chart a course that will influence your entire life! Placing crystals in a grid is a very potent practice in witchcraft. It is a spiritual means to channel energies in a designated direction. Close your eyes for a second and picture a beautiful design you have made with a collection of crystals, all chosen by you because of their qualities and energy resonance. Doesn't the mere idea bring you peace?

It acts as a conduit for you to tap into the latent, secret powers of the Earth and cosmos—harnessing this energy to develop, heal, and change. For these reasons, a crystal grid is a very powerful and intentional arrangement of crystals that come together to help you achieve inner harmony. Think of it as a mini sanctuary, a place of utter peace. Creating this grid can be as simple or complex as you would have it be. Some grids can be made with a few crystals, while others can be much more elaborate. What you make will depend on what you want to manifest. Each of these patterns is connected with sacred geometry, and they are all ways to tap into an entire universe of energy.

Now, when you put these crystals in a grid, their individual energies and vibrational frequencies complement and marry into one another, creating something entirely transformational. Because it is so in tune with energy channeling, the pattern you create when you make a grid is crucial.

Creating a crystal grid does not need to be complicated to work. You simply make it by placing the crystals in a pattern that allows one to feed off the next. Crystal grids are powerful and enable you to harness the energy of crystals thoughtfully and intentionally. A crystal grid is essentially an intentional arrangement of crystals placed to manifest a specific result. Whether you're looking to perform in-person or distance healing, manifest your desires, set intentions, perform ritual work, engage in creative or artistic activity, or simply meditate, crystal grids can be an incredibly effective practice to help you achieve your goals.

Crystal grids can be symmetrical or asymmetrical, combining your intention with crystal energies and sacred geometry. Any crystals that are arranged thoughtfully with a specific intention can be considered a grid. However, it's important to note that an arrangement with no thought and no purpose might not necessarily be considered a grid. By creating a crystal grid, you can forge a deep connection with the universe and harness the fundamental elements of creation. When you intend to create your crystal grid, you're setting the stage for manifesting your dreams, goals, and desires.

I personally love creating crystal grids as part of my ritual work. They're an integral part of my spiritual practice, and I've found they help me focus my energy and intention in an effective way. Whether I'm looking to manifest abundance, connect with my intuition, or simply set the tone for my day, crystal grids have become an essential tool for me. So, if you want to attach more meaning to your spiritual practice, tap into the power of crystals, and manifest your desires, I highly recommend trying crystal grids. There is no end to the healing you'll experience with a bit of intention and some carefully chosen crystals!

The Composition of a Crystal Grid

By now, you already know that the best way to assemble your crystal grid is by following your intuition.

Understanding the basics will help make this easier, so let's take a look!

Most crystal grids have a central stone, some surrounding and amplification stones, and other objects that are aligned with your purpose (McKinnon, 2021). The **center stone** is usually the largest piece in the grid. Alternatively, it can also be the stone with the highest vibrational energy or the stone whose correspondence connects deeply with your intention. It acts as an anchor for divine energy and will serve as your channel of communication for spreading your intentions to the broader universe.

Surrounding stones are other crystals that you arrange in geometric shapes around this center stone. These stones are your grid's modifiers, either enhancing the center stone's intention or complementing it. You can choose any number of stones depending on how simple or intricate you want your grid to be. Additionally, be mindful of how many stones you will need to complete the pattern you've got in mind.

Your crystal grid can also have optional **amplification stones**. The purpose of these stones is to boost the energy of the entire grid. Think of them like satellites, each working to amplify your intention and extend its outer reach. These can be quartz points or tumbles that you place in geometric points between your surrounding stones. Or, you could make a corresponding outer grid for them too! Quartz is excellent for transmitting, amplifying, and strengthening the charge of your crystal grid, making this a neat option to make your grid more powerful!

Besides these optional stones, you can incorporate other **objects of importance** (also optional). These can be pictures, items from nature that align with your spirit—leaves, flowers, petals, and so on, an item from someone you love, or anything that speaks to you (more on this in Chapter Six)! These are a great addition, especially if you are low on crystals. You can also keep a clear quartz crystal and a crystal wand with activation points handy (for activating the grid). Some of us prefer using our pointer fingers to activate the grids. In Chapter Four, we will go into greater detail on this, so hang in there!

Now, remember when I spoke about intention? I'll tell you why it is so important. Imagine you want a grid to harness love. When you go in with this clear intent, you come prepared. You do some research and know that you'll need a crystal—such as rose quartz—that amplifies and honors this emotion. Other pink and purple stones also help build this intention. It's as simple as this—when you do something with your heart and mind set on it, you want to do a good job. You go in with hope and clarity of mind, and trust me, as a fellow crystal witch, these go a long, long way in helping you get to that golden place where life is warm and kind.

We've officially finished Chapter Two! In this chapter, we learned all about sacred geometry and how it has influenced not just our world but the very core of all existence.

We discussed some special sacred geometric shapes that you could use in your witchcraft practice, and we also talked about the importance of going out in nature and opening your eyes and heart to magic. Remember, a sketchbook and a pen will be your best friends when it comes to getting inspired. And don't ever lose that little flame of creativity in your heart. It is essential; it is what will foster your growth. Finally, we also talked about crystal grids and their basic composition. (We'll go into greater detail later in this book.)

In the next chapter, we will discuss color magic, different chakras, and the uses of colored crystals. It is a deeply informative take that will help you set your intentions with more clarity. See you at the turn of the page!

PART TWO
THE ELEMENTS OF A
DEEPLY POWERFUL
CRYSTAL GRID

HARNESS THE NATURAL FREQUENCIES OF COLOR MAGIC

I deeply adore color magic and believe that it is incredibly personal. Everyone has unique associations and experiences with different colors. This makes color magic a very flexible medium to channel and manifest your intentions. I've heard so many beautiful anecdotes about the power of color magic and how it has helped witches connect with their inner selves and manifest their desires. One of my favorite stories involves a witch struggling with writer's block. She decided to work with the color yellow—which is associated with creativity and intellect—and created a ritual in which she surrounded herself with yellow flowers and lit a yellow candle.

To the witch's amazement, she found that the yellow light permeated throughout her mind and unlocked her creativity, allowing her to write freely and without hesitation. Another beautiful aspect of color magic is its accessibility to everyone, regardless of their experience level. Whether you're a seasoned witch or just starting out on your spiritual journey, you can tap into these magical properties to manifest your desires, connect with your inner being, and unlock your creativity by working with the energies and symbolism of different colors. So why not try incorporating some color magic into your practice and see what beautiful things you can manifest?

As always, let us begin at the origin point by understanding the simple mechanics behind this practice.

WHAT IS COLOR MAGIC?

You may not have known this, but in our daily lives, we are always harnessing the subtle powers of colors around us. Think about it. Have you ever gotten ready for a date, looked at several lipstick shades, and thought, "This feels like a red lipstick kind of date?" Often, we associate the color red with confidence, love, and the desire to have fun. And that influences our choices!

Similarly, do you feel yourself drawn to light colors in the summer and darker ones in the colder months? That's your internal consciousness, too, and it already knows different colors have different powers. Some help you feel light and airy, and others come with snuggly comfort.

Color magic happens when you use the spectrum of colors and their intentions to invoke certain responses.

Many of us are already doing it unintentionally, like when we get a fresh arrangement of blue flowers to make a room more airy or red roses for when we want a more decadent, lush feel (Saint Thomas, 2018). Some within the witch family like to draw upon color magic when using candles. Green candles, for example, can help with money spells. Pink can work beautifully for self-love. At the start, it can be overwhelming simply because there are so many colors to choose from! But don't worry because we'll briefly break down how colors work a little later in the chapter. When you do choose a color, feel free to experiment until you find one that resonates with your aura.

CRYSTALS AND THEIR RELATIONSHIP TO CHAKRAS

Now, one of the core reasons why colors are so central to us crystal witches has to do with *chakras*. Chakras represent different energy centers in our bodies. They correspond to specific colors. Therefore, the kind of crystal you choose will always play a significant role in the type of healing you experience. If you can align the hue of your crystal to the matching chakra, you open up the possibility of supercharging your intentions (Anahana, 2022). Crystals that resonate with the color frequency of the chakra you're trying to heal will help harmonize the balance of energies within you.

You could be wondering—what is so important about chakra healing? And how can colors influence this process? Let's delve deeper into this.

Each of us has seven core energy centers within our bodies. These centers are known as chakras. *Chakra* is a Sanskrit term that can be literally translated as "wheel." Within yoga, we use this word to talk about how energy moves throughout our bodies. In other words, the seven chakras are the main energy centers of our bodies (Sugarman, 2021). They correlate with different parts of our health, how we express ourselves, our abilities, and—you guessed it—different colors.

In an ideal situation, all the chakras in our bodies would be unblocked. This means that we'd experience a free flow of energy and complete harmony within our bodies. That's a beautiful way to live if you ask me. Imagine never having thoughts like "I hate myself," "I feel so down and low on energy today," and "Everything sucks." Yes, that sounds pretty idealistic. In real life, most of us experience some form of imbalance in these energy centers.

Our seven chakras are core components of our energetic or *subtle* body. This points to the part that we can't touch or see but always feel. Our chakras do the things that keep us alive, even if we're not consciously aware of them, like making our hearts beat, keeping our intuition intact, and contributing to the energy that forms the very foundation of our physical being. When one or more chakras get blocked, we experience different negatives, such as an overwhelming emotional imbalance that manifests in us feeling lonely, insecure, and afraid (Anahana, 2022). You could also experience physical symptoms like indigestion, headaches, and gut problems. Ultimately, if you feel like your energy is out of whack and you can't relate to anything or anyone around you, it's a sign of a potential blockage in your system.

Chakras can get blocked for many reasons. Usually, this happens because of our fast-paced, unhealthy lifestyles built off of negative thoughts, insufficient physical activity, irregular sleep cycles, and bad diets. Most of us don't know that there are ways in which we can actively restore balance within our systems, and we think that if something is going wrong, the best way to deal with it is to push it down. When we ignore the signs, our chakras can become hypoactive or hyperactive. With the former, your chakra distributes reduced energy. And with the latter, there's far too much energy going around, which also causes imbalance.

We have seven major chakras inside our bodies (Stelter, 2016). Let's briefly go over each of them.

The Root Chakra (Muladhara Chakra)

The root chakra makes its home at the base of the spine and speaks to our deep senses of stability, security, and connection to the physical world. It represents our foundation in terms of our physical existence and emotional well-being. Under balanced circumstances, the root chakra keeps us feeling secure, grounded, and able to handle life's challenges. However, if the root chakra is out of tune, we experience feelings of insecurity, fear, and instability (Stelter, 2016). Imbalances in this chakra may physically manifest as lower back pain, issues with the legs or feet, immune system disorders, or digestive problems.

The Sacral Chakra (Svadhishthana Chakra)

Centered in the lower abdomen, the sacral chakra is the origin point of our creativity, sensuality, and emotional well-being. It governs our ability to experience pleasure, joy, and intimacy. When balanced, this chakra allows us to feel a healthy flow of emotions, a sense of passion and creativity, and the ability to connect deeply with others. Imbalances can result in a lack of creativity, difficulty expressing emotions, or challenges with cultivating and maintaining intimate relationships (Stelter, 2016). Physical imbalances may manifest in the form of lower back pain, reproductive system disorders, or issues with the urinary system.

The Solar Plexus Chakra (Manipura Chakra)

The solar plexus chakra exists in the upper abdomen, near the diaphragm. It represents personal power, confidence, and self-esteem. It is what speaks to our ability to assert ourselves in the world and make decisions with clarity. When in tune and balanced, this chakra keeps us confident, motivated, and capable of achieving our goals. However, imbalances in the solar plexus chakra can lead to a lack of self-esteem, indecisiveness, or a tendency to seek validation from others. Physically, imbalances in this chakra may manifest as digestive issues, adrenal gland disorders, or issues with the pancreas (Hoare, 2020).

The Heart Chakra (Anahata Chakra)

The heart chakra is in the middle of the chest and represents unconditional love, compassion, and psychological health. It shows our capacity for self-love and loving others. Feelings of love, compassion, and oneness arise when the heart chakra is in harmony. An inability to create healthy connections and feelings of loneliness and bitterness might result from an imbalance in this chakra. Heart problems, breathing difficulties, and high blood pressure are some of the physical problems resulting from an unbalanced heart chakra (Yoga Journal, 2021).

The Throat Chakra (Vishuddha Chakra)

The throat chakra is located in our throats and is linked to speech, creativity, and honesty. It stands for the honesty and clarity with which we may express ourselves. When harmonious, it enables us to express ourselves clearly, listen to others with compassion, and openly discuss our innermost ideas and emotions. The inability to express oneself, anxiety about being judged, and emotional repression are all symptoms of an imbalance in the throat chakra. Sore throats, thyroid problems, and strain in the neck and shoulders are just some of the physical symptoms that may result from an unbalanced throat chakra (Sugarman, 2021).

The Third Eye Chakra (Ajna Chakra)

The third eye chakra sits above the brows in the center of the forehead. It's often used to describe one's own innate knowledge, clarity, and intuition. This energy center is symbolic of our non-physical intelligence and perception. Intuition, clear vision, and the capacity to make good choices are all enhanced when the third eye chakra is in harmony. When this chakra is out of tune, we may experience brain fog, indecisiveness, or a loss of touch with our inner wisdom. Third eye chakra imbalances may cause physical symptoms such as headaches, eyestrain, and insomnia (Ahmad, 2021).

The Crown Chakra (Sahastrara Chakra)

The crown chakra is at the very peak of the head, and it is there that we make contact with the spiritual realm and the energy of the universe. It represents the coming together of one's own spirit with the divine. When in harmony, the crown chakra helps us profoundly understand our connection to our spiritual selves and the bigger universe around us. Otherwise, an imbalance can create a situation where you lose touch with your spiritual side and feel like your life has no significance. Physical manifestations include headaches and other neurological problems (Better Sleep, 2022).

Knowing how to unblock your chakras is a prerequisite for maintaining good health and peace of mind. When you're in that Zen state and feel balanced, you'll see that healing comes naturally to you—and this is where color magic comes in. When it comes to chakras, each energy center is often associated with a specific color. These colors are thought to represent each chakra's vibrational frequencies and qualities. For example, the root chakra is often linked to the color red, while the sacral chakra is associated with orange, the solar plexus chakra with yellow, and so on.

When a chakra becomes imbalanced or blocked, it can throw off the natural energy flow within our subtle bodies, affecting our overall well-being. Crystals of corresponding colors can be used as supportive tools to restore balance to these energy centers. Crystals are believed to carry their own energetic properties and vibrations, which can harmonize and align the imbalanced chakras.

For instance, if your root chakra is imbalanced, causing feelings of insecurity or a lack of stability, consider working with crystals like red jasper or garnet. These crystals, with their deep red hues, are said to resonate with the root chakra's core energy and can assist in grounding and bringing a sense of rooted stability to your being. Similarly, if you find your throat chakra is imbalanced, affecting your ability to express yourself authentically, you may choose to explore crystals such as blue lace agate or sodalite. These crystals, with their soothing blue tones, are believed to support clear communication and self-expression, helping you reach deep within to find your voice so you can speak your truth.

It's important to remember that crystal healing is complementary, and the effects can vary from person to person. The crystals serve as energetic allies, working alongside your intention and self-care practices to restore balance to the chakras. And now that we're here, let's explore the different colored crystals and how they can work to align your chakras.

CRYSTAL COLOR MAGIC

Depending on their colors, different crystals can heal specific chakras and restore their energies. We will go over some examples here, but you can get a more detailed outlook on specific crystals in Chapter Seven.

White Crystals

Dalmatian Stone, Danburite, Howlite, Merlinite

First, let's talk about white. White or clear crystals symbolize cleanliness and purity. They help bring pure intentions to your thoughts and actions, generate mental clarity, and do away with the clutter that comes when our own thoughts overburden us. White crystals are suitable for those of us seeking new beginnings. They're also great if you're just starting out because they can be effortless to work and connect with. If you want to bring serenity and peace to your space and enjoy feeling calm and centered, white crystals are your best friends. For me, white crystals help cleanse energies and bring a deep sense of innocence, peace, and vulnerability. I look back at the original implication of the color—white represents the mystical rays of the moon, and, therefore, these crystals are ruled by divine, feminine lunar energy. This is why they are great for anyone who wants to experience tranquility (Tiny Rituals, 2023f). They are a source of inspiration, improved psychic powers, and purpose. They also carry soothing energies that shield you from negative influences and keep you in the presence of the light. These crystals are the key to balancing the **crown chakra.**

Red Crystals

Jasper, Garnet, Carnelian, Ruby, Vanadinite

For all things of the heart, think love, passion, and confidence—the color red is your north star. Red symbolizes the hue of our blood, the planet Mars (which we also relate to the energies of passion and intimacy), and our **root chakra**, which constitutes our basic survival instincts. Therefore, the energy of red crystals is raw, high, and intense. These symbolize passion, energy, and life—making us feel more motivated. If you are emotionally drained, you need red in your life. Red crystals also symbolize courage and willpower, so whenever life tests you and makes you feel unconfident, you know what color you need! The energies of the root chakra can be tapped into with the help of red gems like red jasper or garnet (MyCrystals, n.d.). If this chakra is obstructed or uneven, its vibrational frequencies might assist in unblocking it. People commonly turn to red gemstones for help with centering, stability, and feeling safe in their daily lives.

Pink Crystals

Rose Quartz, Kunzite, Rhodochrosite, Rhodonite

A lighter shade of red, pink is a subtler expression of the more vibrant energies we associate with red crystals. Pink crystals exude warmth, loving, and kind energies but also share the same type of commitment as their red counterparts. What does the idea of pink make you feel? To me, it is a cozy color that warms my heart—and that is the beauty of crystals with this hue! They bear soothing energies that breed compassion and tenderness. They are ideal for forgiveness, self-love, healing, and letting go. If you want to open your heart to abundant love, pink crystals are your go-to option (Energy Muse, 2022). Pink stones connect with the **heart chakra**. When the heart chakra is blocked, their peaceful and loving vibrations may help cure it. Pink crystals are frequently used to aid in developing positive traits, including affection, self-love, understanding, reconciliation, and mental wellness.

Orange Crystals

Amber, Chiastolite, Genesis Stone, Sunstone, Tiger's Eye

Orange represents our **sacral chakra**; therefore, it stands for the human traits of creativity and sexuality. Crystals of this color help bring that spark into our lives, particularly when we need to boost our creative selves! Think of orange crystals as lightning bolts or superfast chargers acting on your inner energy (Young, 2021). They whet your imagination, increase your self-worth, and make you more enthusiastic about life. And who among us doesn't have those days when we'd give anything to feel a little inspired? It turns out all you need is an orange crystal! This color also helps you transition calmly through major life changes without crumbling, and for that, it is affirming and strengthening.

Yellow Crystals

Citrine, Pyrite, Yellow Zircon, Yellow Tourmaline, Yellow Apatite, Yellow Calcite

Yellow reminds me of sunshine, happy days, warm butter on toast, and everything that is bright and happy. Yellow crystals carry the powers of enlightenment, optimism, and willpower. They enable you to find and express your most authentic self, embark on new adventures and relationships, and try out new interests you've always wanted to explore. Yellow is the color that opens your eyes to the new wonders of the universe. On days when we feel weary, it could be just what we need to become more excited about love (Beadnova, 2020). Therefore, yellow-colored crystals are excellent for bringing positivity, energy, and authenticity into our lives. This color is deeply attuned to the **solar plexus chakra** and is the key to connecting with our internal selves, building self-belief, and engendering confidence in our abilities.

Green Crystals

Epidote, Fuchsite, Hiddenite, Moldavite, Unakite

Think nature, money, and newness, and you have the color green. Green can infuse your soul with the power of fresh starts and growth. It can also become the tool via which you attract fortune, prosperity, and greater vigor into your life. Green stands for creation, growth, development, and the beautiful ways in which nature renews itself over and again. It is also a color for stability and helps keep your life balanced. Green crystals boost productivity, foster professional and personal victories, and manifest abundance. As a symbol of fertility, green also helps improve relationships with your loved ones and makes you feel whole on a physical, emotional, and spiritual level. Healing and balancing the **heart chakra** may involve using green gemstones like green aventurine or malachite. These gems aid in facilitating the opening and awakening of the heart chakra due to the balance, nurturing, and restorative vibrations they emit (Satin Crystals,

2023). Green crystals have the power to realign the heart chakra—improving one's emotional health, capacity for forgiveness, and openness to love on all sides.

Blue Crystals

Apatite, Azurite, Chalcedony, Larimar, Rosasite

Blue is such a beautiful color. It reminds me of open skies, a deep ocean, and a sense of freedom and boundlessness. Blue crystals soothe and calm our bodies and minds. They can also help us connect deeply with our inner selves. Blue represents the **throat chakra** and is an excellent color for improving communication and enhancing our abilities to express ourselves. Blue is also the color that helps you stay faithful to your most personal, profound truths when you communicate with the world. It gives you the clarity and strength to speak what you believe in while maintaining a state of calmness and confidence (Shubhanjali, 2022). They are known as crystals of harmony because of their cool tones and ability to keep you sensitive, tender, and thoughtful. In a way, blue crystals—by making you excel at communicating—are essential to healthy, nourishing relationships.

Purple Crystals

Ametrine, Iolite, Sugilite, Tanzanite

Purple is among the most spiritually charged colors, and crystals with this hue are intrinsically connected with the higher chakras, including the **third eye and crown chakras.** They help you rekindle your relationship with your higher self and channel your inner divinity. Purple is also the color of royalty and nobility. It has an element of mystery to it. Crystals of this color are mainly used to open higher chakras and draw you closer to a sense of enlightenment. They help you find your true purpose and can aid in many relaxation and meditation practices. Purple crystals are unique because of their potential to stimulate our spiritual consciousness (Asana, 2022). They may help us relax, increase our psychic abilities, and strengthen our relationship with cosmic forces.

Many people seek out purple crystals for their capacity to improve spiritual experiences, increase mental clarity, and instill a feeling of peacefulness and contentment. When the third eye chakra is balanced with purple crystals, we experience a deeper sense of clarity, direction, and inner wisdom. These crystals may also help us learn about ourselves and our place in the universe.

Black Crystals

Aegirine, Andradite, Apache Tears, Nuummite, Onyx

Black is the most protective color out there. Since ancient times, black crystals have been employed to act as a shield against negativity and bolster mental strength. When you need an extra something to feel more safe and secure, black crystals will show you the way. Black crystals stand for physical safety. They help quell negativities and fears from our surroundings and are also called barrier crystals because of their ability to shield you from harmful energies. Think of them as your bodyguards, working around the clock to keep unwanted elements out of your life.

Black gemstones, such as black tourmaline and obsidian, act as protecting forces that repair and balance the **root chakra**. Black crystals may help us feel more secure and grounded when we put our energy into working with them (Cape Cod Crystals, 2023). They may be utilized to dispel any lingering negativity or emotional barrier that has settled within the root chakra. In addition to providing a feeling of physical and energetic safety, black crystals may act as a barrier against electromagnetic frequencies.

Wasn't that enlightening? So, in this chapter, we learned all about colors, color magic, the seven chakras that form the foundation of your existence, and how crystal colors work to heal them. You now know that all of this is deeply interconnected. When you consider your inner energies, the simplest and most profound truth is that when there is balance, there will be peace. That is what makes crystal magic so wholesome.

At this stage, you now understand the fundamentals of color magic. Each of these colors can come together to protect and balance your energies—especially in the context of crystal magic. Before you move ahead and begin practicing, there are other aspects you will need to consider, including the physical properties of crystals and characteristics like shape and size. We will cover more on this in the next chapter.

CHAPTER 4

DISCOVER THE PHYSICAL CHARACTERISTICS THAT ENHANCE GRID ENERGY

G oing into this chapter, we will learn about the physical nuances of crystals and how they impact their energies' flow and intensity. You will get an idea of what size crystals you need and the most suitable shapes within the context of crystal grids.

CRYSTAL SIZE

A widespread concern among those practicing crystal magic is whether the size of your crystal will impact its energies. The answer is subjective and depends on the kind of grid you are working with. Crystal size becomes important when dealing with a larger grid and when you're trying to affect a significant space with the crystal's energy. But, if you want a small and personal impact, the crystal's size is not a primary concern.

When we think about crystal size, an important consideration is the energy torus. Toroidal (donut-shaped) energy fields surround everything. This includes us, those around us, trees, animals, the Earth, the Sun, and crystals as well. The donut shape of the torus represents the energy flow. It has an energy column that forms its central axis. From here, energy flows out of one vortex and travels into the opposite vortex in one fluid, continuous motion. Imagine a donut surrounding your body. It could be a narrow one, with not too much filling, or it could be a broad and rounder one. This depends on the type of energy flowing through it, but this *flow* will remain the same. As humans, we have one overall energy torus. We also have mini energy tori that exist around each of our chakras.

With crystals, the shape becomes crucial regarding the crystal's energy flow. If the crystal comes with a natural termination point, the energy will be focused at the tip. If the crystal is a sphere, the energy will move evenly in all directions. If you have a piece of selenite, the energy will flow in a vertical line. When you consider the energy torus of small versus large crystals, you will see that a small crystal does not have the same energy torus as its larger counterpart. So, keeping a smaller crystal on your person—in the form of jewelry or even in your wallet—allows you to experience the healing frequencies of the crystal within your own personal energy field.

On the other hand, if you want to work with something more significant—say, changing the energy of a whole room—you will need a larger crystal simply because it has a larger torus. The torus field encompasses larger spaces, such as a room or an outdoor area. This is because the energy of the space extends further and may require a larger crystal to influence and harmonize that expanded energy field effectively. A bigger crystal allows for greater surface area and volume, enhancing its energetic presence and impact within the larger space. Just as a larger musical instrument produces a more resonant sound, a large crystal has the potential to generate a wider energetic presence. Additionally, the larger size of the crystal can create a stronger focal point for intention and energy projection. It can serve as a centerpiece or anchor for the energetic work being done in the space—amplifying and radiating its specific energetic qualities.

It's important to note that the size of the crystal is not the sole determining factor for its effectiveness. The energetic properties, composition, and personal resonance with the crystal also play significant roles in its ability to interact with the energy of the space. Ultimately, using a larger crystal in a larger space allows for a more impactful energetic presence and influence, supporting the intention of harmonizing and balancing the energy within that expanded area. It creates a dynamic interplay between the crystal's inherent properties and the unique energetic qualities of the environment, facilitating a more profound and transformative energetic experience. With all that being said, don't feel obligated to go out there and invest in a large crystal. At the end of the day, you need to employ a crystal that will suit the kind of work you want to do. If the type of healing you seek is within a smaller, centered space, a small crystal will work just fine.

Crystals of the same size will roughly emit the same energy torus. However, there are variations depending on the mineral constitution of the crystals. A rose quartz crystal, for instance, has a smaller energy torus than clear quartz. The extent to which you can sense a crystal's energy torus will vary individually based on your current state and level of sensitivity. For those of us who need more time sensing crystal energy, there could be a more prominent energy blockage that needs to be cleared first. As with anything, you need time and patience before you start feeling the measurable impact of your crystal; remember to give things the room they need to grow.

Don't be disheartened if you're working with other witches and they say they're feeling the energetic vibrations sooner than you. This is a very individual experience, and we have different sensitivities. I, for instance, don't do well with pain. Even a paper cut makes me miserable. That doesn't make me good or bad; it simply means that you and I will have different experiences when it comes to paper cuts. It could take you longer to feel the energy vibrations of your crystal—so give yourself the time needed to hone your craft. At the end of the day, your intention is the most important. Keep that in mind, and amazing things will happen!

You must remember that crystal sizes are only important when considering the size of the area you are looking to impact. The size has nothing to do with one crystal being better. That is, once again, subjective, depending on what works best for you. I resonate with amethysts more than rose quartz, but that is because of the kind of energy I want as a dominant factor in my life. Each crystal has different specialties, and what you experience will largely depend on your *purpose.* **For crystal grids,** you can work with multiple crystal sizes depending on the kind of work you're doing. I prefer to have the central crystal be the largest, but you can keep a small crystal in the middle and surround it with other crystals to amplify the overall energy of the grid. Crystals, when grouped together—as is the case with a grid—will always emit a larger energy torus. The more crystals that make up the grid, the larger the overall energy torus will be. Consider your own self, the space you want to impact, and the best course of action for both.

CRYSTAL SHAPES

When exploring the fascinating world of crystals, it's intriguing to discover how different shapes can influence their energetic properties. Crystal shapes play a significant role in harnessing and directing the energy of these magical stones. We will look into the most popular forms and their impact on energy in relation to crystal grids. Whether you're selecting a center stone or a surrounding stone, any shape can be employed depending on your intentions and what resonates with you. Without further ado, let's delve into the world of crystal shapes!

Before diving into the components of crystal grids, it's essential to touch upon wands and crystal points. These versatile shapes can be utilized for various purposes, including *activating* crystal grids.

Crystal Wands

Crystal wands are sacred tools utilized to activate and harmonize energy within crystal grids. These wands are meticulously crafted from a variety of gemstones, each possessing its own distinct energy signature and metaphysical properties. The gem you choose depends on the specific intention and purpose of the crystal grid. The wand acts as a conductor and energy amplifier when activating a crystal grid. Its elongated shape facilitates focused energy transmission, allowing for the precise targeting of specific crystals or grid points.

The wand's material can play a crucial role in energy dynamics. Clear quartz wands are versatile and highly regarded for their ability to amplify intentions and energies, making them suitable for any grid. Amethyst wands are known for their spiritual and calming properties, ideal for meditation or spiritual growth grids. Rose quartz wands emit gentle, loving vibrations—perfect for grids centered around emotional healing or self-love.

Crystal Points

Crystal points are versatile tools for activating and directing energy within crystal grids. These remarkable formations, characterized by a pointed apex, possess unique metaphysical properties that enhance energy flow. Placing the points strategically within the grid helps establish energetic pathways, encouraging the flow of intentions throughout the crystal matrix.

Crystal points are available in various gemstone varieties, each imbued with distinct qualities. Clear quartz points, known as master healers, are highly sought after for their amplifying and cleansing abilities. Amethyst points promote spiritual growth and intuition, while citrine points stimulate abundance and manifestation. Different gemstone points can be chosen based on the specific intentions and energies one wishes to align within the grid.

ACTIVATING CRYSTAL GRIDS

Crystal wands and points are great for activating crystal grids because of their focused apex that acts as a conduit for directing energy. Their symmetrical shape and termination allow for precise energy targeting, making them practical tools for activating specific crystals or focal points within the grid.

To activate a crystal grid with a wand or crystal point, begin by setting a clear intention and visualizing the desired outcome. With a focused mind, hold the wand or crystal point over the grid and gently touch or hover over the crystals to connect their energy. Start with the center stone and individually connect each stone in the grid back to the center stone, extending outwards in a circular path. This establishes a clear and intentional pathway for the energy to flow, promoting synergy and amplifying the grid's intention.

When choosing center stones and surrounding stones, feel free to work with what you have. The energy and intentions you infuse into the crystals are equally important as their shapes. However, if you have the freedom of choice, here are some top picks for crystal shapes that can enhance your experience.

GOOD PICKS FOR CENTER STONES

Center stones are the foundational stones in a crystal grid that serve as the central focus for intention and energy flow. They are carefully selected based on their unique properties and energetic characteristics to enhance and amplify the desired intentions. These center stones are prominent in the grid, radiating their energy and influencing the surrounding crystals. They act as the core or anchor, providing a robust and energetic foundation for the overall grid.

The selection of center stones is a deliberate process considering various factors, such as the stone's vibrational frequency, color, and metaphysical properties. Each stone carries a distinct energy signature, and selecting the right one for you can greatly enhance the intended purpose of the grid. By carefully selecting center stones, one can create a focal point that aligns with the desired intention: healing, manifestation, spiritual growth, or any other purpose. These stones become the centerpiece of the grid —directing and channeling the energy toward the intended goal. Let us examine some choices for center stones.

Clusters

Clusters are magnificent formations of crystals where multiple points or terminations grow together. These intricate and beautiful formations have unique qualities that contribute to their effectiveness. They exude a magnetic energy that makes them excellent choices as center stones in crystal grids. One of the key reasons why clusters make great center stones is their ability to radiate abundant and expansive energy. The combined power of multiple crystal points creates a powerful synergy. This synergy not only enhances the energy of the center stone but also influences the surrounding crystals, infusing them with amplified vibrations.

Clusters have a remarkable capacity to purify the surrounding environment and energy field. They act as energetic filters, absorbing negative energies and trans-forming them into positive, harmonious vibrations. This cleansing effect promotes a balanced and clear energy flow within the crystal grid, enhancing the overall effectiveness of the intention. Furthermore, the interconnected structure of clusters facilitates a sense of unity and cooperation among the crystals within the grid.

Just as a community thrives on collaboration and mutual support, clusters create an environment that nurtures cooperation and collective growth. They foster a sense of unity and cohesion, ensuring that the energy within the grid remains interconnected and synchronized. Incorporating a cluster as a center stone in crystal grids adds visual beauty and enhances energy dynamics. They provide a profound and transformative energy, promoting purification, unity, and amplification.

Larger Raw/Roughs

Larger raw or rough crystals hold a unique and captivating energy, making them exceptional choices as center stones in crystal grids. With their raw and untamed beauty, these natural formations bring a distinct presence to the grid and offer several advantages over smaller crystals. One notable advantage of using larger raw or rough crystals as center stones is their ability to absorb and emit a stronger energetic presence. Due to their size, they have a greater surface area, allowing them to interact with a larger volume of energy. This amplifies their influence within the grid, making their presence more potent and noticeable.

Moreover, larger raw or rough crystals have a captivating and primal energy. They retain the natural essence of the Earth and carry a sense of ancient wisdom and power. This rawness and authenticity add depth to the energy field of the grid, creating a grounded and profound connection to the Earth's energies. The larger center stone also allows it to act as a focal point, drawing attention and intention toward it. This focal point serves as a visual and energetic centerpiece, enhancing the overall aesthetics and intention of the grid. It becomes the anchor of the grid, commanding attention and guiding the energy flow within the crystal arrangement.

When selecting a larger raw or rough crystal as a center stone, choosing one larger than the surrounding crystals is preferable. This size difference ensures that the center stone absorbs and emits a stronger presence within the grid. It becomes the dominant force, radiating its energy and influencing the surrounding crystals, creating a harmonious and balanced energetic field. Incorporating larger raw or rough crystals as center stones in crystal grids adds visual impact and infuses the grid with potent and primal energy. Their size, authenticity, and commanding presence contribute to the grid's overall effectiveness and transformational power.

Geodes

Geodes are extraordinary formations that capture the imagination with their hidden treasures and captivating beauty. These remarkable geological wonders hold a distinct energy, making them exceptional choices as center stones in crystal grids. When utilizing geodes, their unique qualities contribute to the overall experience in a powerful way.

One of the most remarkable aspects of geodes is their hidden interiors. These hollow cavities within the rock are lined with crystal formations, creating a mesmerizing display of color, texture, and sparkle. This concealed beauty symbolizes the exploration of our inner depths and the discovery of hidden potentials. Incorporating a geode as a center stone in a crystal grid serves as a reminder to explore the depths of our being and uncover the hidden gems within.

The crystals within the geode also work in synergy, creating a unifying energy field. This balanced energy emanates from the geode and permeates the surrounding crystals, promoting coherence and alignment within the grid. It facilitates a sense of unity and equilibrium, creating a stable and supportive environment for energy work and intention setting. Furthermore, geodes have a nurturing and protective quality. They create a safe and sacred space within the crystal grid, shielding and guarding the energy within. The crystal formations within the geode act as a natural filter, purifying and transmuting any negative or stagnant energies, promoting an uplifting and graceful environment.

Incorporating a geode as a center stone adds a sense of wonder to the crystal grid. Its unique beauty and energy become a focal point, drawing attention and intention toward it. This visual centerpiece enhances the grid's overall presence and energetic dynamics, creating a captivating and transformative experience. By embracing the genuine beauty and energy of geodes, we invite the exploration of our inner landscapes and harmonizing energies within the crystal grid.

Pyramids

Pyramids have long captured our fascination with their majestic and timeless allure. These iconic structures hold a profound energy that makes them exceptional choices as center stones in crystal grids. When incorporating pyramids into our practices, their qualities contribute to a genuinely unique experience.

Pyramids are deeply rooted in sacred geometry; their shape is believed to harness and amplify energy—acting as a powerful energy generator. The pointed tip of the pyramid serves as a focal point for intention and energy, facilitating the focused direction and flow of energy within the crystal grid. This directed energy enhances clarity, intention setting, and manifestation. Pyramids also symbolize spiritual growth and transformation. They represent the ascent from the earthly realm to higher states of consciousness. The shape of the pyramid creates a harmonious energy flow, allowing for the channeling of divine energies and the alignment of the mind, body, and spirit. As a center stone in a crystal grid, the pyramid encourages spiritual awakening, inner exploration, and the integration of higher wisdom.

Furthermore, pyramids have a stabilizing and grounding effect. The triangular structure provides a strong and stable foundation, anchoring the energy within the grid. This stability promotes balance, resilience, and a sense of security within the energetic field. The pyramid's grounding energy serves as a supportive force, helping to anchor intentions into the physical realm. Incorporating a pyramid as a center stone in a crystal grid adds a sense of awe and focus. Its distinct shape commands attention and intention, drawing energy towards the apex and radiating it outward. This visual and energetic centerpiece enhances the grid's overall aesthetics and vibrant dynamics, creating a powerful and transformative experience. We embark on spiritual growth, intention manifestation, and grounded transformation by embracing the pyramid's natural energy and symbolism.

Obelisks

The obelisk shape itself holds significance and symbolism dating back to ancient civilizations. It represents a lingering connection between earthly and divine realms, bridging the physical and spiritual planes. The four sides of the obelisk symbolize the four elements—earth, air, fire, and water—creating a harmonious and well-rounded energy. The four sides also stand for stability and balance, working to amplify energy and intention. The pointed tip of the obelisk serves as a focused conduit, directing energy toward a specific goal or purpose. It enhances clarity of intention, aiding in manifestation and spiritual alignment. The energy flow within the crystal grid becomes heightened and directed, allowing for a more potent and purposeful experience.

Four-sided obelisks also possess a commanding presence with their vertical structure, drawing attention and acting as a beacon of light and guidance within the grid. This visual and energetic centerpiece becomes a focal point, anchoring the energy and intentions of the grid while also radiating its influence throughout the surrounding crystals. Incorporating a four-sided obelisk as a center stone in a crystal grid adds an element of grandeur and focus. Its elegant shape and powerful energy create a visually captivating experience, enhancing the grid's overall appeal and energetic dynamics. The obelisk reminds us of our connection to higher realms and the potential for spiritual growth and transformation.

Seer Stones

A seer stone, also known as a window quartz or an ema stone/egg, is a fascinating and enchanting crystal formation with a unique energy, making it an extraordinary choice for crystal grids. Seer stones offer a genuine and powerful experience, carrying the power of insight and clarity within them. The defining feature of a seer stone is its naturally polished and smooth surface, which reveals a translucent window-like area within the crystal. This window acts as a portal to inner wisdom and hidden truths. When gazing into the seer stone, one can embark on a journey of self-discovery, connecting with higher guidance and accessing profound insights.

One of the remarkable qualities of seer stones is their ability to enhance inner vision and intuitive abilities. They are regarded as powerful tools for scrying and divination, enabling the seer to tap into their intuition and receive messages from the spiritual realms. The energy of the seer stone facilitates a deeper connection with one's higher self and the realms of spirit. They create a bridge between the conscious and subconscious mind, promoting deep introspection and the exploration of one's inner landscape. Holding or meditating with a seer stone can open the third eye chakra, allowing for enhanced clarity, spiritual perception, and the development of psychic gifts.

Seer stones possess a calming and grounding energy. They offer stability and presence, allowing for a clear, focused mind during divination or meditation. The gentle energy of the seer stone promotes relaxation, balance, and inner harmony, creating a supportive and conducive environment for intuitive exploration. Incorporating a seer stone into a crystal grid adds an element of insight and introspection. Its unique energy becomes a focal point, drawing focus and intention toward inner wisdom and spiritual guidance. This visual and energetic centerpiece enhances the grid's overall look and feel, creating an engaging, life-changing experience. By embracing the seer stones' natural energy and wisdom, we embark on a journey of self-discovery and spiritual connection.

Other than these center stone options, you could also be interested in a specific center stone shape if your intention is more definite. Let's take a look at some of these unique shapes.

Crystal Hearts

Heart-shaped center stones hold a unique energy that calls to the heart chakra. They serve as powerful reminders to cultivate self-love, deepen connections with others, and nurture emotional well-being. Heart-shaped stones emanate a gentle and nurturing energy that encourages the release of emotional blockages, facilitating emotional healing. Incorporating crystal hearts into your grid fosters a sense of forgiveness, harmony, and balance.

Crystal Eggs

Egg-shaped center stones hold a unique energy that symbolizes rebirth, transformation, and new beginnings. Just as a chick emerges from its egg, these stones represent the potential for growth and evolution. They bridge the divide between the past and future, offering balance and harmony. Egg-shaped stones serve as catalysts for personal transformation, encouraging us to break free from our old ways and embrace positive change. Their smooth, nurturing energy resonates with the root and sacral chakras, grounding us in the present moment and igniting creative energy.

Crystal Skulls

Skull-shaped center stones hold a perceptive energy that helps us explore the depths of our consciousness and embrace the concept of impermanence. The skull shape symbolizes the cycle of life, death, and rebirth, reminding us of the preciousness of every moment. Skull-shaped stones serve as potent tools for introspection, shadow work, and spiritual growth. They encourage us to confront our fears, release limiting beliefs, and embrace our authentic selves. The energy of skull-shaped stones resonates with the crown and third eye chakras, facilitating heightened intuition, expanded awareness, and connection to higher realms.

Crystal Spheres

Sphere-shaped center stones embody unity, harmony, and balance. Their symmetrical shape radiates energy equally in all directions, promoting a sense of wholeness and interconnectedness. Spheres facilitate energy circulation, enhance meditation, and create a harmonious environment within crystal grids.

Crystal Angels

Angel-shaped center stones carry gentle and uplifting energy, evoking qualities of divine guidance, protection, and compassion. Their form serves as a reminder of angelic presence and spiritual support. Angel-shaped stones nurture a connection to higher realms, encourage healing, and infuse crystal grids with loving and benevolent energies.

Platonic Solids

Due to their sacred geometrical significance and powerful energetic properties, platonic solids make great center stones in crystal grids. There are a total of five platonic solids, each with its own unique properties and energetic qualities. As center stones, they anchor and amplify the intentions of the grid, creating a focused energy field.

Tetrahedron

The tetrahedron, representing fire, embodies dynamic energy, creativity, and transformation. Its triangular faces symbolize harmony and balance. When used as a center stone, tetrahedron-shaped crystals ignite passion, catalyze personal growth, and empower the manifestation of desires. They infuse the grid with vibrant energy and motivate the pursuit of dreams.

Hexahedron (Cube)

The cube, representing the earth element, provides stability, structure, and grounding. With its solid and symmetrical nature, cube-shaped stones establish a firm foundation within the grid. They manifest intentions, bring clarity, and foster a sense of security. Cube center stones emanate practical and organized energy, promoting productivity and stability in pursuing goals.

Octahedron

The octahedron symbolizes air and brings balance, harmony, and spiritual growth. Its dualistic nature represents the interconnectedness of all things. Octahedron-shaped crystals serve as center stones to facilitate inner equilibrium, emotional healing, and enhanced spiritual connections. They inspire deep insights, harmonize relationships, and infuse the grid with a sense of serenity and spiritual expansion.

Dodecahedron

The dodecahedron has strong links with the element of ether or spirit. It embodies divine wisdom, cosmic consciousness, and the interconnectedness of all creation. As a center stone, dodecahedron-shaped crystals assist in accessing higher knowledge, fostering spiritual growth, and connecting with higher realms. They radiate a profound energy that expands awareness, promotes unity, and invites transformative experiences within the grid.

Icosahedron

The icosahedron represents the water element and symbolizes emotional healing, adaptability, and transformation. Its fluid geometry inspires creativity and encourages positive change. Centering the grid with an icosahedron-shaped crystal enhances emotional balance, intuition, and fluidity in various aspects of life. These stones promote a free flow of emotions, support adaptability to life's challenges, and bring forth a refreshing energy that revitalizes and rejuvenates.

One harnesses these unique qualities by incorporating these distinctive platonic solid center stones into crystal grids, creating a synergistic and empowered environment for intention setting, healing, and spiritual exploration.

That covers your center stones. Now, let's do a deep dive into the surrounding stones and what could be ideal options for them!

GOOD PICKS FOR SURROUNDING STONES

We already know what these are, but let's briefly recap. Surrounding stones play a crucial role in crystal grids, complementing the center stone and enhancing the overall energy and intention of the grid. These stones encircle the central focus, creating a supportive, harmonious, energetic field. Surrounding stones are carefully selected based on their energetic properties, colors, and correspondences to amplify specific intentions or address particular areas of healing. They serve to expand and diffuse the energy radiated by the center stone throughout the grid, creating a balanced and coherent vibration. Surrounding stones can be chosen intuitively or based on their unique metaphysical qualities to enhance the crystal grid's overall energy flow and effectiveness. Let's take a look at some great options for these stones.

Smaller Raw/Rough Stones

Smaller raw or rough stones are excellent choices as surrounding stones in crystal grids, offering natural and supporting energy to complement the larger center stone. When placed around a larger center stone, smaller raw and roughs provide a solid foundational energy that supports and enhances the intentions of the grid. In their natural and unpolished form, these smaller stones directly connect to the Earth's energy. They possess a pure and untamed essence that aligns with the primal forces of nature. These raw stones act as conduits, channeling the

Earth's energy and infusing it into the grid. Their rough texture and unrefined appearance create a distinct contrast, adding depth and character to the overall aesthetic of the grid. Smaller raw and rough stones bring a sense of groundedness, stability, and authenticity to the grid, reinforcing its energy and intention.

The combination of a larger center stone and smaller raw or roughs forms a symbiotic relationship. In this context, the center stone receives support and empowerment from the surrounding stones, while the raw stones benefit from the focused energy of the central intention. Furthermore, these surrounding stones act as amplifiers, magnifying the energy emitted by the larger center stone. They create a cohesive, interconnected, energetic network within the grid, facilitating a harmonious energy flow throughout the crystal layout. Incorporating smaller raw and rough stones as surrounding elements in a crystal grid adds an earthy and primal element to the overall energy dynamics. With their raw supporting energy, these smaller stones contribute to the holistic and organic power of the grid, providing a solid foundation for the manifestation of intentions and the overall energetic experience. Their untamed nature connects us to the natural world, reminding us of our innate connection to the Earth's wisdom.

Tumbled Stones

Tumbled stones are a wonderful choice as surrounding stones in crystal grids. They offer a smooth, polished energy that harmonizes with the larger center stone. As surrounding stones, tumbled stones provide a gentle and balanced energy that complements and supports the intentions of the grid. These stones undergo the process of tumbling, where they are polished to reveal their inherent beauty and enhance their energetic qualities.

The smooth surface of tumbled stones creates a soothing and inviting presence within the crystal grid. Their polished appearance enhances their aesthetic appeal and represents a sense of refinement and transformation. Tumbled stones carry a refined energy that resonates with harmony and balance, creating a serene atmosphere within the grid. Tumbled stones act as bridges when placed around a larger center stone, facilitating energy flow between the center stone and the surrounding elements. They help to distribute the energy evenly throughout the grid, ensuring a coherent and balanced vibration. The polished surface of tumbled stones also assists in releasing any stagnant or negative energies, promoting a clear and vibrant energy field within the grid.

Additionally, tumbled stones offer a nurturing and comforting energy that promotes emotional well-being and healing. Their smooth texture and rounded shapes evoke a sense of calmness and reassurance, creating a supportive environment for personal growth and transformation. By incorporating tumbled stones as surrounding elements in a crystal grid, one invites a gentle and polished energy that complements and enhances the intentions of the larger center stone. Their refined nature and harmonizing qualities contribute to the grid's overall energy flow and effectiveness, creating a balanced and inviting energetic space for healing, manifestation, and spiritual exploration.

Crystal Points

Crystal points are an excellent choice as surrounding stones in crystal grids, offering a focused and directed energy that amplifies the intentions of the larger center stone. With their distinctive shape, crystal points serve as energetic antennas, transmitting and receiving energy in a precise and concentrated manner. When placed around a larger center stone, crystal points create a dynamic energy flow within the grid. Their pointed ends act as conduits, directing energy toward the tip while radiating outward energy to harmonize and balance the grid. This focused energy enhances the intention-setting process and supports the manifestation of desires. The sharp end of a crystal point can be likened to a laser beam, cutting through energetic blockages and facilitating the release of stagnant or negative energy. This purifying quality helps maintain the clarity and vibrancy of the grid's energy field.

Furthermore, crystal points can enhance the connection with higher realms and spiritual guidance. They bridge the physical and spiritual realms, facilitating communication and opening channels for intuitive insights and spiritual growth. In addition to their energetic properties, the striking appearance of crystal points adds visual appeal to the grid. Their geometric elegance and radiant presence create a visually captivating and energetically vibrant environment. As surrounding stones in a crystal grid, crystal points emit focused and directed energy, aligning and empowering the intentions of the larger center stone. Their precise and amplifying qualities contribute to the overall energy dynamics of the grid, creating a potent and transformative energetic space for healing, manifestation, and spiritual exploration.

Crystal Double Points

Finally, double points, also known as twin or double-terminated points, possess a balanced energy that facilitates flow in both directions. Double points act as connectors, linking and balancing the energies within the grid. When placed around a larger center stone, double points create a continuous and uninterrupted energy flow, enhancing the synergy and coherence of the grid. Their double terminations allow for the simultaneous transmission and reception of energy, promoting cooperative exchanges and balanced vibrations.

Double points also symbolize unity and connection, representing the interconnectedness of all things. Their presence in a crystal grid fosters a sense of wholeness, integration, and alignment on both physical and energetic levels. Incorporating double points as surrounding stones amplifies the intentions of the center stone while facilitating the harmonization of energies within the grid. Their balanced and versatile energy promotes balanced growth, fulfilling relationships, and a deeper understanding of the interconnected nature of existence.

When choosing your crystals for your grid, you are now armed with everything you need to know about different crystal shapes! Remember that intention, purpose, and patience are your watchwords, which will keep your practice golden. Moving forward into the next chapter, we will discuss the whimsical practice of combining different crystals so that you can harness opposing powers to one harmonious end.

CHAPTER 5

CULTIVATING SYNERGY THROUGH CRYSTAL COMBINATIONS

In this chapter, we will explore the realm of crystal combinations, where the magic of synergy awaits. We will unveil the profound effects of merging crystals, revealing the transformative potential that lies within their collaboration. Brace yourself for an exploration of starter suggestions that ignite sparks of inspiration as we demystify the art of pairing crystals and unveil how effortlessly you can master this ancient technique. Without further ado, let's get into it!

WHAT ARE CRYSTAL COMBINATIONS?

Crystal combinations are a captivating exploration of the dynamic interplay between multiple crystals, where the unique energies of each crystal harmoniously merge to create a unified and potent force. Delving into the world of crystal pairings unlocks endless possibilities for healing, manifestation, and spiritual growth. When selecting crystals for combination, it is essential to consider their individual properties, metaphysical qualities, and vibrational frequencies. By carefully curating these pairings, we can tap into the collective wisdom and power of the crystals, magnifying their effects and creating a synergistic energy field.

Each crystal possesses its distinct energetic signature, resonating with specific intentions and aspects of wellbeing. When brought together, these crystals can enhance and support each other's properties, forming a powerful union that aligns with our desired goals. For example, combining the calming energy of amethyst with the purifying properties of clear quartz can create a potent synergy that promotes spiritual clarity and inner peace.

Merging the energies of different crystals into one coherent whole offers a wonderful opportunity to explore the intricate relationships between crystals, unlocking hidden connections and uncovering new insights. Some crystals have natural affinities and work exceptionally well together, such as rose quartz and green aventurine, which combine to create a graceful blend of love, healing, and abundance. It's important to approach crystal combinations with intuition and intention, allowing the energies of the crystals to guide the process. By listening to our inner wisdom, we can intuitively sense which crystals complement and amplify each other, creating a balanced and coherent energy field.

FACTORS TO CONSIDER WHEN CHOOSING CRYSTAL COMBINATIONS

When venturing into crystal combinations, clarifying your intention for the crystal grid or spell is essential. Define your desired outcome and identify the areas of your life or well-being that require attention. This clear intention will guide you as you navigate crystal combinations. Numerous crystals possess unique healing properties that directly align with specific solutions. Explore the metaphysical attributes of different crystals and select those that resonate with your intentions. Don't hesitate to combine multiple crystal types in your grid, allowing for a rich interplay of energies. Many crystals exhibit versatile properties, enabling them to contribute to various aspects of your desired outcome.

If you are new to crystal witchcraft, you may feel uncertain about approaching crystal combinations. Start by working with crystals that intuitively draw you in, even if you're unsure of their specific properties. Through hands-on experience, you'll discover the unique ways different crystals interact and influence the energy of your crystal grid. Embrace experimentation, and don't be afraid to trust your intuition. The true magic lies in your connection with the crystals. As you handle each crystal, hold it close to your heart and visualize your intentions flowing into the stone. Infuse it with your energy and purpose. This personal touch will enhance the energetic bond between you and the crystal, amplifying its impact within the grid.

Remember that their energies harmonize rather than cancel each other out when combining crystals with seemingly conflicting qualities. It's like blending different colors to create a vibrant masterpiece. For instance, pairing a calming crystal with one that promotes motivation may result in giving you focus, creating a well-rounded energy dynamic within your grid. It is also essential for you to visualize the outcome you want from your grid. For instance, maybe you want an interplay of energy and clarity. You might desire clarity to get a picture of where you need to go and the energy to actually get there. This could be your angle when it comes to choosing crystal combinations. If the situation demands, you can build a crystal grid with a particular type of crystal. This will come with the benefit of performing spells with one crystal, and the spells will also be supercharged because of the powers of your grid. Truly, the options are vast and entirely in your hands.

Trust the synergistic effects of crystal combinations as they work in unison to manifest your intentions. As you gain confidence and expertise in working with crystal combinations, you'll naturally begin to sense the unique energetic qualities of each crystal and how they interact within the grid. You'll better understand the subtle shifts and influences that occur. This awareness empowers you to adjust and fine-tune the energies within your crystal grid to align with your evolving intentions. There are no rigid rules when it comes to crystal combinations. Embrace your journey of exploration and self-discovery. Allow yourself to experiment and witness the beautiful dance of energies within your crystal grid. Trust in your ability to intuitively select and arrange crystals that feel right to you. The magic is in your hands, and as you weave together the energies of different crystals, you unlock your immense potential and create a powerful tapestry of manifestation.

At the end of the day, we sometimes work better when we have multiple perspectives coming together, and sometimes we just need a singular direction. Your intuition will never disappoint you—especially when it is trying to speak to you. Use it to determine how to move forward.

ALTERNATIVE IDEAS FOR CHOOSING CRYSTAL COMBINATIONS

When you choose combinations for your crystal grids, you can be influenced by several factors. Some may draw you in because of how well the colors work together. Some may have a distinct kind of energy that speaks to them. Let's briefly explore this topic.

Color Magic

Color plays a significant role in the world of crystals, and consciously utilizing it can enhance the potency of your crystal combinations. Each color carries its own unique vibration and corresponds to specific energies and intentions. Incorporating color into your crystal combinations allows you to create harmonious and synergistic energy dynamics within your crystal grids or spells. Consider the intentions and energies you wish to invoke. For instance, if you seek love and emotional healing, you may choose to combine pink and green crystals. Pink represents unconditional love, compassion, and self-care, while green signifies growth, balance, and heart-centered healing. The combined energies of these colors work in unison, amplifying the intentions and manifesting the desired outcomes.

Similarly, combining crystals in shades of indigo and purple can be beneficial for enhancing intuition and spiritual growth. Indigo, representing the third eye chakra, promotes intuition and insight, while purple embodies spiritual connection and higher consciousness. This combination establishes a powerful energy field that supports your spiritual journey and expands your intuitive abilities. Remember that color associations can vary based on personal interpretations and cultural symbolism. Trust your intuition and emotional resonance when working with colors in crystal combinations. Explore the nuances and energetic qualities of different color combinations and their effects on your intentions and well-being.

While color is a guiding principle in crystal combinations, it's important to note that crystals hold multifaceted properties beyond their color associations. Each crystal possesses a unique metaphysical essence that extends beyond its visual appearance. Therefore, consider the crystals' color and inherent properties when creating combinations. Embrace your creativity and experiment with different color combinations. There are no rigid rules, and you can explore and discover new synergies between crystals. Follow your inner guidance, and trust that your chosen colors will contribute to your crystal combinations' overall energy and resonance.

Chakras

As we previously discussed, chakras are powerful energy centers that correspond to different components of our physical, emotional, and spiritual well-being. By aligning crystals with specific chakras, we can create harmonious and balanced energy flows within our crystal grids. To begin harnessing the power of chakras in crystal combinations, it's essential to understand the energy centers and their associated colors.

For instance, we may choose to combine red crystals like red jasper and garnet to balance and energize the root chakra. These crystals help ground our energy, provide stability, and address issues related to survival and physical well-being. Similarly, if we seek to stimulate the heart chakra, we may opt for green and/or pink crystals like green aventurine or rose quartz. These crystals promote love, compassion, and emotional healing, supporting our ability to give and receive love unconditionally. When creating a crystal grid, we can strategically place the grid in the surrounding space that we frequent, for example. This alignment encourages energy flow through the corresponding chakras, restoring balance and vitality.

It's important to note that while aligning crystals with specific chakras is beneficial, they also possess unique properties and energies that extend beyond color associations. Therefore, consider both the color and inherent properties of crystals when combining them for chakra-focused grids. Trust your intuition and personal resonance as you explore crystal combinations with chakras. Intuitively select crystals that resonate with the energy of each chakra and place them with intention and mindfulness in your crystal grid. Allow yourself to experiment and discover the synergies between crystals and chakras that work best for you. Working with crystals aligned with the chakras in your crystal combinations can facilitate deep healing, energetic alignment, and spiritual growth.

Zodiac Signs

With their distinct energies and characteristics, the zodiac signs can be a powerful guide when creating crystal combinations. Each zodiac sign is associated with specific elements, ruling planets, and personality traits. By aligning crystals that resonate with the energies of different zodiac signs, we can enhance our spiritual practice, tap into cosmic energies, and deepen our self-understanding.

Before incorporating the zodiac into crystal combinations, consider the elemental correspondences associated with each zodiac sign. For example, fire signs like Aries, Leo, and Sagittarius are linked to the element of fire, which represents passion, creativity, and transformation. Crystals such as carnelian, citrine, and garnet, which carry fiery energies, can complement and amplify the traits of these signs. Water signs, including Cancer, Scorpio, and Pisces, symbolize emotions, intuition, and deep sensitivity. Crystals like amethyst, moonstone, and aquamarine resonate with the water energy, facilitating emotional healing and spiritual connection.

Air signs such as Gemini, Libra, and Aquarius embody intellectual pursuits, communication, and the power of the mind. Crystals like clear quartz, blue lace agate, and labradorite, which promote mental clarity and communication, can enhance the energies of these signs. Earth signs, including Taurus, Virgo, and Capricorn, are grounded, practical, and connected to the physical realm. Crystals like green aventurine, smoky quartz, and jasper, which carry grounding and stabilizing energies, can harmonize with the earthy qualities of these signs.

To create crystal combinations aligned with the zodiac, choose crystals that resonate with your zodiac sign or those of others you wish to support. You can also consider the ruling planets and birth charts to refine your crystal choices further. Experiment with different crystal combinations and observe how they enhance your connection with the energies of specific zodiac signs. Combining zodiac signs with crystal combinations adds a celestial dimension to your spiritual practice. It deepens your understanding of yourself, strengthens your connection to the universe, and invites cosmic energies into your journey of self-discovery and personal growth.

The Main Elements

When we think of the main elements, we have earth, air, fire, and water. There are crystals that work well with each of these elements and their energies. Stones that work beautifully with air include selenite, fluorite, amethyst, labradorite, and sugilite. Crystals that resonate with fire are carnelian, amber, fire opal, red jasper, and sunstone. The earth element can be amplified with crystals like jade, agate, hematite, jasper, onyx, obsidian, black tourmaline, pyrite, and garnet. Water stones include pearl, selenite, rose quartz, moonstone, aquamarine, and amethyst.

Remember that fire works beautifully when paired with air when making these combinations. Likewise, earth and water are a stable, solid marriage. You can also combine two crystals from the same elemental family, further boosting their shared elemental prowess. It is important to note that "conflicting" elements work the same way as two seemingly opposing traits. In the context of a crystal grid or spell, when two crystals with otherwise opposing characteristics are brought together through programming and intention, they seek to work together as you are granted benefits from both sides. Again, trust your inner intuition with this. The answer will naturally come to you in terms of what's best for harmonic wholesomeness.

Crystal Families

You can work with complementing energies and receive their amplified advantages if you use crystal families to make your combinations. Begin by familiarizing yourself with different crystal families like amethyst, quartz, tourmaline, or citrine. Each family will come with unique characteristics. Once you know the shared qualities, choose complementary crystals for your grid's intention. You can look for harmonious contrasts—like colors or formations that pair well. When you combine crystals from the same family, you build a synergy that amplifies the energies of your grid. For instance, you can combine different quartz crystals if you want clarity.

The quartz family includes rose and clear quartz, citrine, and amethyst, among others. The feldspar family comprises stones like labradorite, moonstone, and sunstone. The calcite family has vibrant crystals in colors like blue, green, and orange and is beautiful for mental clarity and emotional healing. The tourmaline family comprises pink, black, and green tourmaline, among others. These crystals are wonderful for protection, support, and grounding. If you seek balance and inner harmony, you can combine crystals in the agate family, including blue lace, moss, and banded agate. The options are entirely limitless, so don't be afraid to try and experiment with the crystal families until you find something that resonates with your purpose.

Crystal Structures

Crystal structures can help when it comes to determining fluid combinations. For example, cubic or isometric crystals have a square inner structure. Crystals within this group would include combinations like diamond, fluorite, garnet, and pyrite. Similarly, hexagon crystals have a six-sided internal structure and include stones like aquamarine, apatite, and emerald. Calcite and hematite belong to the rhombohedral system comprising triangular inner structures. Consider your intentions when it comes to combining crystals based on their structures. You can combine cubic crystals to amplify stability, grounding, and manifestation powers. Similarly, combining hexagonal crystals enhances spiritual growth and mental clarity.

Intuition

Above all, use your inner intuitiveness when it comes to combining crystals. When you have different crystals in your hands, you will see that some feel naturally complementary while others don't. Crystal healing is a very *individual* craft, and a combination that works wonders for someone else may not necessarily do so for you. The opposite is equally valid. You may find that combining citrine with rose quartz brings you immense healing. Someone else may not reap the same benefits. At these times, intuition will serve to guide and show you the way. Allow yourself the kindness of exploring and experimenting, and you *will* find something that resonates with you.

Combinations Based on Ailments

Each crystal carries unique properties and energies that can support healing and well-being. When it comes to combining crystals for ailments, there are various approaches you can explore. Here are some general examples of crystal combinations for specific ailments:

Stress and Anxiety

Amethyst & Rose Quartz

Combining amethyst and rose quartz can help ease stress and promote relaxation. Amethyst aids in calming the mind and enhancing spiritual connection, while rose quartz brings soothing energy and encourages self-love.

Sleep Issues

Lepidolite & Selenite

Lepidolite and selenite can be a powerful combination for improving sleep. Lepidolite helps to reduce anxiety and promote tranquility, while selenite has a calming effect and can cleanse and purify the energy in your sleep space.

Digestive Problems

Citrine & Yellow Jasper

Citrine and yellow jasper can support digestive health. Citrine stimulates the digestive system and encourages vitality, while yellow jasper provides grounding energy and aids in balancing the digestive system.

Emotional Healing

Rhodonite & Labradorite

Combining rhodonite and labradorite can assist in emotional healing. Rhodonite promotes forgiveness and emotional balance, while labradorite helps to release negative emotions and enhance inner strength.

Focus and Concentration

Clear Quartz & Fluorite

Clear quartz and fluorite can aid in improving focus and concentration. Clear quartz amplifies clarity and mental focus, while fluorite enhances cognitive abilities and promotes mental organization.

Remember, these are just general examples, and the choice of crystals ultimately depends on individual preferences and intuition. When combining crystals for ailments, it's important to connect with the energy of each crystal and trust your instincts.

We will discuss more about the specificities of different crystals in Chapter Seven. For now, my advice is to trust in the greatness of your mind and heart. At the onset, the idea of falling back on your instincts may be over-whelming—but don't overthink it. Here's a secret: Life is all about the present moment. Once you open yourself to the beauty of experiment and discovery, the world will start revealing secrets you never deemed possible.

There are endless combinations, and you're good as long as you have one that speaks to you. With that, we wrap up this chapter. We discussed crystal combinations, what could work, and what factors to consider when choosing your gemstones. In the next chapter, we'll discuss how you can elevate your magical practice by maintaining an energetically safe space.

United by Energy, United by Words

"We have what we need, if we use what we have."—Edgar Cahn

We're all bound together by energy. This is what gives us our power. It's what allows us to use crystals for healing and make waves in the world around us.

Perhaps you were born into a witchy family; perhaps you came to witchcraft through your search to find answers about the world around you; maybe magic came to you before you really understood what it meant... No matter how you got here, you're on a voyage of discovery. You're aware of your internal power, and you're aware of the power held within others.

And that puts you in a unique position to help those who are discovering more on their path. The energy we have within us is the energy we put out into the world, and while much of that is done simply with intention and focus, as you know by now, there are tools we can use to help us.

There's one tool that's far less mystical than the crystal, however, a tool that the human race has been using for thousands of years: the written language.

Through the written word, we can go beyond sharing energy: We can share information. And that's crucial if we want to help other people find the guidance they need to help them on their spiritual journey.

By leaving a review of this book on Amazon, you can help people unlock their inner power and discover the secrets of crystal grids.

Visit the link below or scan the QR code to leave your review on Amazon.

https://cosmiccompendiums.com/review

Simply by sharing how this book has helped you and what information you found here, you'll help other readers find the guidance they seek.

Your energy is powerful, but it's not the only tool you have to help others. Thank you for joining me on my mission to spread the word!

CHAPTER 6

UPGRADING THE VIBE BY MAINTAINING AN ENERGETICALLY SAFE SPACE

This chapter is all about elevating your magical practice. You will learn to reap the maximum benefits from your practice by keeping a space that is energetically safe and feels like shelter. We will discuss sanctuaries, altars, and items with distinct energy and spells, along with their numerous benefits so that you create the best, most nourishing space for your healing work to commence.

The first and natural question you'll have is, why do I need a sacred space? To begin with, building this space will infuse your spirit with a lasting sense of peace and cleansing energy.

You will learn the workings of dedicated cleansing crystals and stations, incense, spiritual music, and protected spaces. In doing this, you will imbibe a natural urge to safeguard yourself and keep your energy pure. Remember, we are going into this with the hope of building intent. When you surround yourself with the intent of working in a safe haven, it leaves a lasting impact on your spellwork.

You may not need to cleanse your crystals too often when you're already in a pure space; you may only need to cleanse them when you're prepping them for a new grid or spell (we will cover cleansing in more detail in Chapter Nine). With a designated space, it's also easier to regulate the type of energy you'll allow inside, which helps you let go of everything that does not serve you. There's this beautiful philosophy I deeply believe in, and I learned it from a line by Pablo Neruda. He once said that we should, with generosity, learn to forget those who cannot love us. This is the spirit I want for you.

The grace of letting go includes the urge to understand that when you protect your space, you don't necessarily stop loving others, but you also love yourself enough to know where your limits lie. This is you being the keeper of your heart. You deserve that kind of self-love.

A practical benefit of a dedicated space is that you save a lot in prep time and organization. There are fewer distractions and more personalization; these benefits allow you the freedom to delve deeper into your practice.

Now, you might think you'll need a massive, grand area to set up your sacred space, but don't worry. It's not about the square feet you devote here. Instead, focus on the intention you're carrying to a space that's just snug enough for you, your grid, and your practice. This could be a small corner in your bedroom, study, living room, or terrace—anywhere you'll have a bit of peace and quiet. The most important thing here is consistency, so whatever space you choose, stick to it. Over time, when you keep going back to one place to practice, you'll find that the natural energy of this place resonates deeply with you because it has built up to become your ideal safe space. It will soothe you the second you enter it because your subconscious already knows where it belongs.

Establishing a sacred space allows you to connect with your innermost self. By designating a room or area separate from the distractions of your home and the outside world, you create a haven that allows you to focus on embracing your authentic essence. Strive for simplicity when you're curating this space. Remember, the external environment often mirrors our internal state, so if the sacred space feels cluttered, it is a soft reminder that you may be juggling too many commitments and should consider slowing down the busy pace of your life.

PERSONAL RITUAL SPACE

Irrespective of your religious beliefs, having a sacred space is essential to pause, reflect, and unplug from the daily grind the world exposes us to. It gives you time to focus on the more important things—loving life, being grateful, and nourishing your soul with some self-adoration. A designated space for meditation and spellwork is a reminder that the world is large, beautiful, and magical to the eyes that go beyond superficiality (Rosebud Woman, 2021).

Your personal ritual space should leave you feeling tranquil and rejuvenated whenever you emerge. It should be a place you enter, surrounded by protective energy that builds up over time. When you fill an area with good intentions, it will be nothing but golden over time. The spells you conduct here will have residual effects, which will spill over and make your work and results more impactful. The cleansing energy of this space should keep your grid pure, allow you to have a deep connection with your larger existence, and *make you feel like you're in the arms of pure, safe love.* You can use it for worship, divination, reaching out to the universe, self-care—you name it.

Personal Sanctuary

Before making your personal space, consider the intention you're going with. What is your purpose? Are you seeking a connection with your higher self or looking to ground your aura with nature? For the latter, a little spot in a garden or balcony could work wonders. For the former, you could simply choose a quiet zone in your bedroom or study, maybe by a window.

Be creative. Maybe your space is limited, but that doesn't need to affect your practice. Look for corners that are being left unused. You could also use makeshift partitions —think billowy curtains or, in my case, a pillow fort I used to hide inside as a child! Fill this space with things that make your heart warm. Your sacred space can be as big as the ocean or simply your favorite chair. It could even be a pillow! What matters is the intention you set around this space. If your pillow is sacred to you, simply carrying it around will give you a feeling of safety and purpose.

Use all your senses. What appeals to your eyes, ears, taste, smell, and touch? I love the lingering scent of jasmine and colors like white and lavender. I adore sitting down with a mint in my mouth and letting it dissolve before I begin my spellwork. And I like to feel the Earth beneath me when I practice. These define the kind of space I work in. Choose what makes your soul sing, and every day will make you happier. Your space should be somewhere that makes you *want* to keep coming back—even if it's just for ten minutes a day.

When selecting your sanctuary, consider avoiding areas:

- with high foot traffic (to maintain a sense of tranquility)
- that are associated with your job
- where you do chores
- where you attend to practical matters like paying bills

To begin your sacred journey within this sanctuary, cleanse the space to create a pure and sacred atmosphere (again, this will be covered in Chapter Nine). This allows you to go in with pure intention and renewed energy. You can employ various methods like smoke cleansing, using sound vibrations, or incorporating cleansing crystals such as clear quartz and selenite. Additionally, engage in meditation, visualization, or breathwork to infuse the space with your intentions and align the energy with your desired state.

Altars

Altars, traditionally associated with religious practices, can also serve as powerful tools for spiritual and self-care rituals. They can become an excellent supplement to your energetic sanctuary and even function as a personal ritual space in their own right, should you desire. An altar provides a dedicated space to focus your intentions and create a more structured ritual setup.

To build your altar:

1. Begin by clarifying its purpose.
2. Determine whether it will primarily be used for meditation, performing rituals, or organizing your witchcraft tools and trinkets.
3. With this intention in mind, select an elevated surface that can be entirely dedicated to the contents of your altar. It could be a nightstand, a shelf, or a table—whatever suits your space and preferences.

Consider incorporating a main feature item on your altar, placed in the center and raised higher than the rest. This item should represent the primary intention of your altar, serving as a focal point. It could be a symbol, an artifact, a crystal, or a cherished object that embodies your desired energy and resonates with your practice.

When incorporating crystals into your altar, infuse the feature piece with your intention by charging it with the specific energy you seek to amplify in your rituals. Clear quartz and selenite are excellent choices to include on your altar, as they provide cleansing and purifying energy. You can also incorporate a smaller crystal cleansing bowl or bag to hold and cleanse your crystals when needed.

Let your creativity shine when decorating your altar with crystals that speak to you. Choose crystals that are attuned to your intentions and enhance the energy you wish to cultivate. You might arrange them in a visually appealing pattern or intuitively place them based on their energetic properties. Feel free to experiment and let your intuition guide you.

When building a crystal grid on your altar, select crystals that complement each other and form a geometric pattern, amplifying the energy of your intentions. Allow the synergy of the crystals to enhance the power of your rituals and manifest your desired outcomes. We will cover this further in Chapter Ten.

Enchanting Your Sanctuary or Altar through Your Senses

When it comes time to enchant your sanctuary, altar, or ritual space, the best thing to do is trust your gut. Be creative. You can choose any number of colors, patterns, textures, scents, lighting, artwork, and magical items. The idea is that the whole you create should calm and rejuvenate you, so with this in mind, feel free to let your creative spirit shine. For sanctuaries, you can choose any decor that compliments or adds to the atmosphere you're looking to build. For altars, focus on sacred items that are personal or hold deep meaning for you—include more objects that you'd actively use in your ritual work.

Incorporating smoke cleansing tools, sound cleansing instruments, and a sea salt or rice cleansing bowl can significantly enhance the energy and purification of your sacred spaces. For smoke cleansing, ignite sage bundles or palo santo sticks, allowing the smoke to waft through the area, carrying away stagnant energy. Sound cleansing can be achieved by using bells, singing bowls, or chimes to produce resonant tones that cleanse and harmonize the environment. A cleansing bowl filled with sea salt or rice can be placed on your altar or in corners of the room to absorb negative energy. Regularly cleanse your space to maintain a sacred and vibrant atmosphere.

Consider incorporating symbolic additions that hold significance and contribute to the desired energy and vibe (referred to as *objects of importance* in Chapter Two). These can include sentimental objects, nature-inspired elements, and items that resonate with your intentions. Start by utilizing things you already own.

Trust your intuition when decorating the space, and follow what feels right. Some examples of symbolic additions are mementos, crystals (for decoration, spellwork, or enchanted purposes), photos, vision boards, postcards, travel souvenirs, plants, statues, books, prayer beads, incense, bells, journals, essential oils, items from nature, wind chimes, and tarot cards. These objects can synergize with your intentions, offering an added effect and serving as substitutes or complements to crystals.

Engage multiple senses to enhance the atmosphere, such as using incense or candles, playing high-frequency music or calming sounds, and enjoying a soothing cup of herbal tea. Don't overthink it—let your inner wisdom guide you in selecting and arranging items that align with the energy and ambiance you seek for your sacred space.

In the next chapter, we will break down some of the best crystals you can use for your grid. By the end of it, you'll be spoiled for options!

PART THREE
THE FOUNDATION
OF ALL CRYSTAL
GRIDS

CHAPTER 7

65+ CRYSTAL PROFILES TO BUILD OUT YOUR GRID

BEFORE WE BEGIN

F inding crystals is an adventure that awaits you in metaphysical shops, online platforms, and even while taking a leisurely walk. Some states and nature parks offer specific crystals, while festivals and fairs devoted to the metaphysical realm unveil various options. When purchasing online, choose reputable sources that guarantee quality and offer return policies.

Metaphysical shops, also known as New Age shops, cater to witchcraft and the broader New Age movement. Here, you'll find a diverse selection of crystals to examine and connect with personally. Remember that other hands may have touched these crystals, infusing them with various energies.

While shopping, it's crucial to prioritize ethically sourced crystals. Inquire about fair wages, working conditions, environmental impact, and the absence of child labor in the crystal mining process. Responsible retailers should provide transparent answers, aligning with the growing concern for fair labor practices and environmental sustainability (more about this in Chapter Eight).

Working with nature necessitates mindfulness and gratitude. When crystals are mined under unfair conditions, we can feel the impact in our hands as we hold them. Building your collection should be deliberate, allowing you to connect deeply with each crystal's energy. Try to resist the temptation to accumulate numerous crystals at once, instead focusing on one or a few gems, dedicating time to bond and program them with intention.

Approach crystal acquisition with a purpose for specific rituals, spellwork, or energy center alignment. Occasionally, you may encounter additional crystals that resonate with you, warranting their inclusion. By adopting a mindful approach, you cultivate lasting connections and harness the full potential of each crystal.

In your journey with crystals, let your intuition guide you. Embrace the wonders of nature and cherish the treasures it bestows upon us, ensuring that your collection grows with intention and appreciation. May your path be adorned with the blessings and transformative energies these remarkable crystals offer.

Moving forward, you will find that each crystal is associated with a specific **element.** Here's what the elemental energies denote:

1. Air represents communication, intellect, and the realm of the mind. It is associated with mental clarity, creativity, and the ability to adapt and flow. Air energy is often linked to thought processes, inspiration, and the power of the spoken and written word.

2. Earth symbolizes stability, grounding, and practicality. It is connected to the physical realm, abundance, and the nurturing qualities of nature. Earth energy promotes a sense of security, strength, and the manifestation of goals and desires.

3. Fire embodies passion, transformation, and the power of energy and action. It represents creativity, vitality, and courage. Fire energy is associated with motivation, personal power, and the ability to initiate change and pursue one's passions.

4. Water signifies emotions, intuition, and the subconscious realm. It represents adaptability, purification, and the flow of energy. Water energy fosters emotional healing, intuition, and a deep connection with one's feelings and inner wisdom.

It's important to note that these interpretations may vary across different belief systems and practices. Cultural, spiritual, and personal perspectives can also influence the energies associated with elements.

You will also notice that suggested cleansing methods are listed for each crystal. If you aren't familiar with that, more will be covered in Chapter Nine! Please note that there are many different ways to cleanse every crystal. Feel free to research further and utilize the tools you currently have available!

Let us now discuss some wonderful crystals for amplifying your practice.

Aegirine

Aegirine derives its name from *Aegir*, the Norse god of the sea, due to its association with oceanic energy. It was discovered in Norway in 1835. As such, it can be found in Norway, Greenland, Russia, and Canada. Aegirine often occurs in alkaline igneous rocks, pegmatites, and metamorphic rocks. To cleanse aegirine, keep it in sunlight for about an hour so the sun's energy can rejuvenate and recharge it. Avoid cleansing methods involving water immersion for more than 20 minutes, as it may not be necessary and could cause erosion over time.

Physical, Emotional, and Spiritual Healing Properties:

- supports the immune system, aids detoxification, and promotes overall vitality
- enhances stamina, reduces fatigue, and supports the adrenal glands
- instills courage, grit, and resilience, helping one overcome challenges and promote assertiveness
- aligns with the energy of the sea, fostering a connection to the ocean's vast wisdom and strength

Zodiac Sign: Taurus

Chakra Alignment: root

Color(s): dark brown, green, and black

Elemental Alignment: earth

Crystal Family: pyroxene

Crystal Structure: Aegirine crystals form in a prismatic or needle-like shape with elongated columnar structures. It showcases a monoclinic crystal system with distinct cleavage planes.

Agate

Agate has a rich history and has been highly valued for centuries. It comes from the Greek word *Achates*, referring to the Achates River in Sicily, where agate was first discovered. It can be found in Brazil, Uruguay, India, Mexico, and the United States. Agate crystals are best cleansed with flowing water. It can also be purified with salt or by being immersed in soil overnight. Avoid leaving the stone in the sun for too long because this can cause the colors to erode and fade.

Physical, Emotional, and Spiritual Healing Properties:

- provides stability, balance, and grounding energy
- promotes inner strength, courage, and self-confidence
- brings harmony, soothes emotional tension, and fosters a sense of peace
- protects, enhances spiritual growth, and promotes mental clarity

Zodiac Sign:

- Blue Lace Agate: Pisces and Gemini
- Moss Agate: Virgo and Gemini
- Fire Agate: Aries and Gemini
- Crazy Lace Agate: Gemini
- Botswana Agate: Scorpio and Gemini
- Black Agate: Gemini

Chakra Alignment:

- Blue Lace Agate: throat
- Moss Agate: heart

- Fire Agate: root, sacral, and solar plexus
- Crazy Lace Agate: all chakras, particularly crown
- Botswana Agate: root
- Black Agate: root

Color(s):

- Blue Lace Agate: delicate light blue and white bands
- Moss Agate: green color and moss-like inclusions
- Fire Agate: mesmerizing play of fiery colors, including iridescent red, orange, and brown tones
- Crazy Lace Agate: vibrant, swirling patterns of various colors
- Botswana Agate: subtle and soothing shades of gray, often with beautiful banding patterns
- Black Agate: predominantly black

Elemental Alignment:

- Blue Lace Agate: water and air
- Moss Agate: earth
- Fire Agate: fire
- Crazy Lace Agate: earth and fire
- Botswana Agate: earth and fire
- Black Agate: earth

Crystal Family: belongs to the quartz family, specifically chalcedony

Crystal Structure: trigonal, belonging to the hexagonal crystal system

Amazonite

Amazonite derives its name from the Amazon River in South America, though it is not found in the Amazon region. Historically, it was associated with ancient Amazonian warrior women. It can be found in Russia, Brazil, Madagascar, and the United States. To cleanse amazonite, try smudging with sage. Avoid using saltwater or exposure to prolonged sunlight, as it may cause color fading.

Physical, Emotional, and Spiritual Healing Properties:

- helps alleviate stress, anxiety, and emotional trauma
- promotes harmony, balance, and clear communication

Zodiac Sign: Virgo

Chakra Alignment: heart and throat

Color(s): light green, ranging from pale green to vibrant turquoise

Elemental Alignment: water

Crystal Family: feldspar

Crystal Structure: triclinic

Amber

Amber has been cherished for its beauty and healing abilities for thousands of years. It is derived from the Arabic word *Anbar*, meaning ambergris. It can be found in the Baltic region, the Dominican Republic, Mexico, and Myanmar. Amber may discolor from exposure to light and is vulnerable to chemical degradation. To cleanse, try using sound—an energetic chant works well with this crystal!

Physical, Emotional, and Spiritual Healing Properties:

- brings warmth, vitality, and positive energy
- soothes physical ailments, enhances creativity, and promotes emotional well-being
- cleanses and purifies energies

Zodiac Sign: Leo

Chakra Alignment: solar plexus

Color(s): warm golden, orange, or reddish-brown

Elemental Alignment: fire

Crystal Family: organic gemstone formed from fossilized tree resin

Crystal Structure: amorphous

Amethyst

Amethyst has been revered for its beauty and spiritual properties for centuries. Its name comes from the Greek word *amethystos* when it was believed to act as a safeguard from intoxication. It can be found in Brazil, Uruguay, Russia, South Africa, and the United States. The best way to cleanse amethyst is with warm water and mild soap. Avoid exposing it to excessive heat or prolonged sunlight, as it may cause fading of its vibrant purple color.

Physical, Emotional, and Spiritual Healing Properties:

- has calming and purifying energy
- promotes spiritual growth, inner peace, and protection against negative influences
- associated with emotional balance, stress relief, and enhancing intuition and psychic abilities

Zodiac Sign: Pisces

Chakra Alignment: third eye and crown

Color(s): pale lilac to deep purple, with some specimens displaying color zoning or variations

Elemental Alignment: air

Crystal Family: quartz

Crystal Structure: hexagonal

Ametrine

Ametrine is a fascinating crystal with a rich history and carries the combined properties of amethyst and citrine. Its discovery dates back to the 17th century in the Anahi Mine in Bolivia, which remains the primary source of high-quality ametrine specimens. When cleansing, use gentle methods such as moonlight bathing (leave it in a bowl of water on the windowsill by a full moon), smudging, or placing it on a bed of cleansing crystals like clear quartz or selenite are also suitable options. Avoid saltwater or harsh chemical cleansers, which may damage the crystal or affect its energetic properties.

Physical, Emotional, and Spiritual Healing Properties:

- promotes mental clarity, enhances creativity, and stimulates the mind
- supports the immune system, aids in detoxification, and helps with fatigue and energy levels
- brings balance, calmness, and optimism, helping to overcome negative emotions using self-acceptance
- fosters spiritual growth, intuition, and connection with higher realms

Zodiac Sign: Libra

Chakra Alignment: crown and solar plexus

Color(s): lighter pastel shades to more vibrant and saturated tones, reflecting the blending of amethyst and citrine

Elemental Alignment: air and fire

Crystal Family: quartz

Crystal Structure: hexagonal

Andradite

Andradite owes its nomenclature to José Bonifácio de Andrada e Silva, who first discovered this mineral in the early 19th century. It occurs in metamorphic rocks and can be found in Russia, Italy, Mexico, and the United States. Cleansing options such as moonlight bathing or placing it on a bed of cleansing crystals like hematite or black tourmaline are suitable. Be sure to avoid exposing andradite to harsh chemicals or prolonged sunlight as it may affect its color or energetic vibration.

Physical, Emotional, and Spiritual Healing Properties:

- promotes vitality, strength, and overall physical well-being
- bolsters the immune system, enhances stamina, and aids in the recovery from illness or physical exertion
- brings courage, confidence, and a sense of empowerment

- helps release self-limiting beliefs, overcome obstacles, and ignite passion and motivation
- grounds, stabilizes, and helps connect with the Earth's energy

Zodiac Sign:

- Melanite: Scorpio
- Demantoid: Leo, Aquarius
- Topazolite: All

Chakra Alignment:

- Melanite: root
- Demantoid: heart
- Topazolite: solar plexus

Color(s):

- Melanite: brownish-black
- Demantoid: deep, vivid green
- Topazolite: a lovely yellowish-green

Elemental Alignment: earth

Crystal Family: garnet

Crystal Structure: cubic

Apache Tears

Apache Tears, named after a Native American legend, possess various physical, emotional, and spiritual healing properties. These obsidian nodules, originating from volcanic ash, are named for the grief and tears shed by the Apache tribe when they were driven from their land. They can be found in the United States, Mexico, and Australia. To cleanse Apache Tears, the best option is simply to hold the crystal under running water. Remember to avoid exposure to extreme temperatures or harsh chemicals.

Physical, Emotional, and Spiritual Healing Properties:

- provides protection and grounding
- alleviates symptoms of grief, trauma, and emotional pain
- helps release negative emotions, promotes emotional healing, and supports inner strength and resilience

Zodiac Sign: Scorpio

Chakra Alignment: root

Color(s): deep black

Elemental Alignment: earth

Crystal Family: obsidian

Crystal Structure: amorphous

Apatite

Apatite's origins lie in the Greek word *apate*, meaning deception, due to its ability to mimic other gemstones. It was named by Abraham Werner, a German geologist, in 1786 and is found in Brazil, Mexico, Russia, and Madagascar. You can cleanse this crystal with breathwork and/or visualization and meditation. Never use steamers, hot water, or ultrasonic cleaners.

Physical, Emotional, and Spiritual Healing Properties:

- supports healthy bones, teeth, and cartilage
- helps manage and balance weight management and metabolism
- enhances motivation, creativity, and self-expression
- alleviates apathy and promotes a sense of clarity and focus
- brings spiritual growth and inner peace
- enhances intuition and psychic abilities, aiding in communication with higher realms and spirit guides
- facilitates past-life exploration and healing

Color(s): blue, green, yellow, and brown (blue apatite, in particular, is highly regarded for its metaphysical properties and is commonly used in spiritual practices)

Zodiac Sign: Gemini

Chakra Alignment:

- Blue Apatite: throat and third eye
- Green Apatite: primarily heart, but also throat and third eye
- Yellow Apatite: solar plexus
- Brown Apatite: root

Elemental Alignment:

- Blue Apatite: air
- Green Apatite: earth
- Yellow Apatite: fire
- Brown Apatite: earth

Crystal Family: phosphate

Crystal Structure: can vary, including hexagonal, prismatic, and tabular formations

Aquamarine

Aquamarine, as its name suggests, is a crystal associated with the calming and soothing energies of the sea. The name aquamarine is from the Latin words *aqua* and *mare*, meaning water and sea. It can be found in Brazil, Madagascar, and Africa. You can cleanse it by smudging. To do this, pass the aquamarine through the smoke of cleansing herbs like sage or palo santo. The smoke helps clear any negative energies surrounding the stone.

Remember to avoid using harsh chemicals or exposing the aquamarine to direct sunlight for long periods, as it may cause fading or damage.

Physical, Emotional, and Spiritual Healing Properties:

- supports the respiratory system, aids in hormonal balance, and promotes overall well-being
- facilitates clear and compassionate communication skills and assists in resolving conflicts
- soothes anxiety and promotes emotional stability
- enhances intuition, meditation, and connection with the divine

Zodiac Sign: Pisces, Scorpio, and Gemini

Chakra Alignment: throat

Color(s): pale blue to deep turquoise

Elemental Alignment: water

Crystal Family: beryl

Crystal Structure: hexagonal

Aventurine

Aventurine originates from the Italian word *aventura*, meaning chance or luck, due to its association with good fortune. It can be found in Brazil, India, Russia, and South Africa. Aventurine does best when being cleansed or charged surrounded by healthy plants. This crystal does not do well when left in the sun or when submerged in water for too long.

Physical, Emotional, and Spiritual Healing Properties:

- supports overall well-being, vitality, and physical healing
- encourages a healthy flow of energy and aids in recovery from illness or injury
- helps alleviate stress and calms the nervous system
- draws luck, prosperity, and success while promoting a positive mindset
- helps release negative patterns, enhancing self-confidence

Zodiac Sign: Aries and Virgo

Chakra Alignment: heart

Color(s): green to various shades of blue and brown

Elemental Alignment: earth

Crystal Family: quartz

Crystal Structure: hexagonal

Azurite

Azurite is a crystal with a long history and powerful metaphysical properties. Its name is from the Persian word *lazhward,* meaning blue, which reflects its striking deep blue color. It can be found in Australia, Chile, China, and the United States. For cleansing, start by gently wiping it with a soft cloth. Then, place it on a bed of quartz crystals or in a bowl of dry rice for a few hours. Alternatively, cleanse it by smudging. Avoid exposing it to water or any harsh chemicals.

Physical, Emotional, and Spiritual Healing Properties:

- supports the respiratory system and enhances overall vitality
- detoxifies and aids in releasing negative energies from the body
- awakens psychic abilities and enhances intuition
- encourages introspection, self-reflection, and the release of limiting beliefs
- helps with spiritual guidance and expansion
- deepens meditation practices and enhances spiritual insights
- facilitates communication with spirit guides and supports astral travel and lucid dreaming

Zodiac Sign: Aquarius and Sagittarius

Chakra Alignment: throat and third eye

Color(s): deep, rich blue, often accompanied by intricate patterns of green or dark mineral inclusions

Elemental Alignment: water

Crystal Family: carbonate

Crystal Structure: prismatic

Bloodstone

Bloodstone's name is derived from the deep red or brown spots on its surface, resembling drops of blood. Historically, bloodstone has been associated with courage, strength, and vitality. Warriors and athletes often carried it as a talisman for protection and endurance during battles or physical challenges. In ancient times, people thought it bore mystical properties, including stopping bleeding and warding off evil spirits. Bloodstones can be found in India, Brazil, Australia, and the United States. It may be easily maintained by rinsing in warm water. While spring water is ideal for many crystals, you may use whatever kind of water you choose. For a more thorough cleansing process, you may bury your bloodstone and allow Mother Nature to do the heavy lifting of extracting the negative energy.

Physical, Emotional, and Spiritual Healing Properties:

- grounds and revitalizes
- supports blood circulation, detoxification, and overall physical vitality
- boosts our immune system and assists in the healing of wounds or illnesses
- associated with courage, resilience, and emotional balance

- helps alleviate stress, promotes inner strength, and enhances self-confidence
- fosters a sense of calm and clarity
- enhances intuition, spiritual growth, and protection against negative energies

Zodiac Sign: Aries, Pisces, and Libra

Chakra Alignment: root

Color(s): deep green to dark green with red or brown spots

Elemental Alignment: earth

Crystal Family: chalcedony

Crystal Structure: cryptocrystalline

Cacoxenite

Cacoxenite originates from the Greek word meaning "Evil or Unwanted Guest," possibly due to its past association as an impurity found in iron ore. However, when presented as beautiful golden strands within larger crystals, it is highly regarded and welcomed for its ability to enhance the gem's properties, making it even more magnificent. It is known as the *stone of ascension* and can be found in Brazil, Madagascar, and the United States. It is commonly found as golden or brownish needle-like inclusions within quartz, amethyst, and other minerals. Cacoxenite can be cleansed by placing it in a bowl of dry sea salt or using smudging techniques with sage or palo santo. It is important to avoid exposing it to harsh chemicals to prevent potential damage.

Physical, Emotional, and Spiritual Healing Properties:

- has a cleansing and energizing effect on the body
- supports the immune system, enhances vitality, and promotes overall well-being
- brings joy, positivity, and spiritual growth
- stimulates optimism, increases self-confidence, and fosters a sense of purpose
- enhances intuition, psychic abilities, and spiritual connection

Zodiac Sign: Aries, Leo, and Sagittarius

Chakra Alignment: crown

Color(s): reddish-orange, greenish-yellow, golden or brownish

Elemental Alignment: fire

Crystal Family: does not belong to a specific crystal family but is instead an inclusion within other crystals like quartz and amethyst

Crystal Structure: hexagonal

Calcite

Calcite is a versatile and abundant mineral that has been employed throughout history for its beauty and meta-physical properties. Calcite gets its name from *calx* (Latin), meaning *lime*, reflecting its abundance in limestone and marble formations. It can be found in various locations worldwide, including Mexico, the United States, Brazil, China, and Iceland. It is commonly found in sedimentary rocks and forms in crystalline masses, rhombohedral or scalenohedral crystals, and stalactites. Calcite can be cleansed by burying it in brown rice for forty-eight hours or passing it through the smoke generated from burning sage. Avoid exposing calcite to harsh chemicals or sunlight.

Physical, Emotional, and Spiritual Healing Properties:

- supports the skeletal system, aids in digestion, and promotes overall physical well-being
- balances the body's calcium levels and supports healthy bone and teeth development
- releases emotional blockages and enhances joy and optimism
- amplifies and cleanses energy, enhances spiritual development, stimulates intuition, and facilitates communication with higher realms

Zodiac Sign:

- Clear Calcite: Cancer
- White Calcite: Cancer
- Yellow Calcite: Leo
- Orange Calcite: Cancer and Leo
- Blue Calcite: Cancer and Pisces
- Green Calcite: Cancer and Taurus
- Pink Calcite: Cancer and Libra

Chakra Alignment:

- Clear Calcite: all
- White Calcite: crown
- Yellow Calcite: solar plexus
- Orange Calcite: sacral and solar plexus
- Blue Calcite: throat and third eye
- Green Calcite: heart
- Pink Calcite: heart

Elemental Alignment:

- Clear Calcite: air and fire
- White Calcite: water
- Yellow Calcite: fire
- Orange Calcite: fire
- Blue Calcite: air and fire
- Green Calcite: all
- Pink Calcite: water

Crystal Family: carbonate

Crystal Structure: trigonal, often forming in rhombohedral or scalenohedral shapes

Carnelian

Carnelian is a vibrant and energizing crystal treasured for its beauty and metaphysical properties throughout history. Its name is derived from *carneus*, meaning *flesh* in Latin. This is due to its warm reddish-orange color reminiscent of the sunset. Carnelian can be found in various locations worldwide, including Brazil, India, Madagascar, and the United States. It is a form of chalcedony and belongs to the quartz family. Carnelian can be cleansed using a solution of mild soap and warm water. Additionally, recharging carnelian by placing it on a bed of hematite or carnelian crystals can be beneficial.

Physical, Emotional, and Spiritual Healing Properties:

- boosts vitality, stimulates metabolism, and supports the reproductive system
- enhances physical endurance, promotes healthy circulation, and alleviates symptoms related to menstrual discomfort
- promotes courage, motivation, and creativity. It inspires confidence and self-expression and helps dispel doubt or negativity

- balances emotions, enhances manifestation abilities, stimulates spiritual growth, and activates intuition

Zodiac Sign: Aries

Chakra Alignment: sacral

Color(s): carnelian comes in various shades of orange, ranging from pale peach to deep reddish-brown

Elemental Alignment: fire

Crystal Family: carnelian is a form of chalcedony and belongs to the quartz family

Crystal Structure: hexagonal

Celestite

Celestite, also known as celestine, is a captivating crystal renowned for its celestial blue hues and calming energy. It gets its name from *caelestis* (Latin), meaning *heavenly* or *celestial*, reflecting its ethereal appearance. It can be found in Brazil, Mexico, and the United States. Celestite is best cleansed by the moonlight. Avoid leaving it in the sunlight for too long, as the color may fade. Due to its delicate nature, handle celestite with care to avoid cleaving or breaking.

Physical, Emotional, and Spiritual Healing Properties:

- alleviates tension, promotes relaxation, and supports restful sleep
- brings stillness, tranquility, and emotional healing, promoting a sense of inner peace and reducing stress and anxiety

Zodiac Sign: Gemini and Libra

Chakra Alignment: throat and third eye

Color(s): typically displays a delicate blue color, ranging from pale sky blue to deeper shades of blue, reflecting its calming and soothing energies

Elemental Alignment: air

Crystal Family: barite

Crystal Structure: celestite typically forms in geodes or crystal clusters

Chalcedony

Chalcedony is a versatile and nurturing crystal valued for its gentle energy and beautiful range of colors. Its name is inspired by the ancient Greek city of Chalcedon, where it was believed to have been first discovered. It can be found in Brazil, India, Madagascar, and the United States. It is cleansed through gentle methods such as running water, moonlight, or sound cleansing. Avoid exposing chalcedony to harsh chemicals or prolonged sunlight.

Physical, Emotional, and Spiritual Healing Properties:

- promotes overall well-being, supports the immune system, and enhances vitality
- known to alleviate throat symptoms and respiratory issues, aid in the absorption of nutrients, and improve digestion
- a stone of harmony and emotional balance, helping to soothe feelings of stress, anger, and anxiety
- encourages a sense of peace, self-acceptance, and inner reflection
- enhances communication, fosters positive relationships, and facilitates emotional stability

Zodiac Sign: Cancer and Sagittarius

Chakra Alignment:

- Blue Chalcedony: throat and third eye
- Pink Chalcedony: heart
- White Chalcedony: crown
- Grey Chalcedony: root
- Green Chalcedony: heart

Elemental Alignment:

- Blue Chalcedony: water
- Pink Chalcedony: water, air, and earth
- White Chalcedony: earth
- Grey Chalcedony: earth and air
- Green Chalcedony: water and air

Crystal Family: quartz

Crystal Structure: hexagonal

Chiastolite

Chiastolite is a unique and fascinating crystal known for its distinctive cross-shaped pattern that naturally occurs within its structure. The name Chiastolite originates from the Greek *chiastos*, meaning "marked with a cross," referring to its characteristic appearance. It can be found in Spain, Russia, and the United States. To cleanse Chiastolite, start by gently wiping it with a microfiber or any soft, clean cloth to get rid of dust. You can then keep it in a bowl of dry sea salt overnight to absorb any negative energies. Alternatively, use smudging with sage to cleanse it. Avoid exposing Chiastolite to water or harsh chemicals.

Physical, Emotional, and Spiritual Healing Properties:

- believed to have physical grounding and protective properties and is included in talismans to ward off negativity and promote stability and balance
- associated with physical healing, particularly in improving and supporting the immune and nervous systems
- emotionally calming and harmonizing
- helps to alleviate stress, anxiety, and negative thought patterns, promoting a sense of peace and emotional well-being
- encourages adaptability, inner strength, and the ability to overcome challenges

Zodiac Sign: Libra and Capricorn

Chakra Alignment: root and third eye

Color(s): brown, black, and gray

Elemental Alignment: earth

Crystal Family: andalusite, a mineral belonging to the aluminum silicate family

Crystal Structure: orthorhombic

Citrine

Citrine is a radiant and energizing crystal known for its sunny yellow color. Its name comes from the word *citron* (French), meaning *lemon*, which perfectly describes its vibrant hue. It can be found in Russia, Brazil, Madagascar, and the United States. Cleanse citrine with warm, soapy water. Prolonged exposure to sunlight may cause its vibrant color to fade over time.

Physical, Emotional, and Spiritual Healing Properties:

- associated with vitality and abundance
- enhances physical stamina, supports digestion, and promotes well-being
- often used to stimulate the metabolism, boost the immune system, and alleviate symptoms related to hormonal imbalances
- helps to dispel negativity, release fears, and encourage a positive mindset
- used to overcome depression, increase self-esteem, and attract success and abundance

Zodiac Sign: Sagittarius, Aries, Leo, and Cancer

Chakra Alignment: solar plexus

Color(s): primarily known for its vibrant yellow color, which could be anything from pale yellow to deep golden

Elemental Alignment: fire

Crystal Family: quartz

Crystal Structure: hexagonal

Creedite

Creedite is a rare crystal named after its discoverer, William Creed. It is characterized by its delicate, elongated prismatic crystals that can form in vibrant clusters and can be found in Mexico. Due to its delicate nature, creedite should be handled with care to avoid damage or breakage. Cleanse it by smudging it with sage. Remember to always source your smudging herbs ethically and be mindful of cultural sensitivities surrounding specific subtypes like white sage and palo santo.

Physical, Emotional, and Spiritual Healing Properties:

- strengthens the immune system and helps with vitamin assimilation
- assists with the healing process, including recovery from injuries like torn muscles
- is said to regulate the heartbeat and help in detoxifying blood (Crystal Vaults, 2023a)
- a powerful crystal for spiritual growth, transformation, and connection to higher dimensions
- enhances intuition, expands consciousness, and facilitates profound spiritual experiences
- helps connect with spiritual guides and angelic realms

- can be used to cleanse other crystals

Zodiac Sign: Virgo

Chakra Alignment: sacral, third eye, and crown

Color(s): white, clear, pink, orange, and purple

Elemental Alignment: air

Crystal Family: sulfate

Crystal Structure: monoclinic, forming in prismatic or tabular structures

Dalmatian Stone

Dalmatian Stone, or Dalmatian Jasper, is a unique and striking crystal named after its resemblance to the black and white spots of the Dalmatian breed of dogs. It is found in Mexico, India, Brazil, and the United States. The best way to cleanse this crystal is with a soft cloth and warm water with a drop of mild soap.

Physical, Emotional, and Spiritual Healing Properties:

- has grounding and protective properties
- balances the physical body's energies, supports the nervous system, and improves coordination and reflexes
- aids in the removal of toxins and promoting overall well-being

- helps to alleviate stress, anxiety, and emotional imbalances, promoting a sense of serenity and joy
- encourages playfulness, positivity, and a childlike sense of wonder, allowing you to let go of negative patterns and embrace a more lighthearted approach to life

Zodiac Sign: Virgo

Chakra Alignment: root and sacral

Color(s): black and white

Elemental Alignment: earth

Crystal Family: chalcedony

Crystal Structure: igneous rock

Danburite

Danburite is a beautiful and high-vibrational crystal named after the town of Danbury, Connecticut, where it was first discovered. It can be found in Mexico, Japan, Russia, Madagascar, and the United States. Cleanse it with a soft cloth, mild soap, and a warm water solution. Avoid exposing danburite to extended hours of sunlight.

Physical, Emotional, and Spiritual Healing Properties:

- believed to have gentle healing properties
- aids in releasing tension and stress
- supports the overall well-being of the physical body, promoting relaxation and assisting in the assimilation of nutrients
- helps to alleviate anxiety, fear, and emotional blockages, promoting a sense of peace and emotional balance
- encourages self-love, acceptance, and the release of emotional trauma, allowing for healing and personal growth
- enhances intuition, psychic abilities, and spiritual communication, assisting individuals on their spiritual path and supporting spiritual awakening and enlightenment

Zodiac Sign: Leo

Chakra Alignment: crown and heart

Color(s): typically colorless or pale pink in its natural form but can also occur in shades of yellow, brown, or gray due to impurities or inclusions

Elemental Alignment: air

Crystal Family: silicate

Crystal Structure: orthorhombic

Diamond

Diamond is a highly prized and cherished gemstone known for its exceptional brilliance and hardness. Carbon atoms in a crystal lattice structure create dazzling optical properties that form a diamond. It can be found in Africa, Australia, Russia, Canada, and Brazil. Using gentle methods such as a soft microfiber cloth and a mild soap solution are suitable for cleansing diamonds. As one of the hardest gemstones, diamond is highly durable but should still be handled carefully to avoid scratches or damage.

Physical, Emotional, and Spiritual Healing Properties:

- associated with strength, endurance, and vitality
- has purifying properties, supporting the overall well-being of the physical body
- enhances the immune system, promotes cellular regeneration, and boosts energy levels
- amplifies emotions and can enhance feelings of love, joy, and abundance while also promoting clarity and mental focus
- encourages emotional balance, self-confidence, and a positive outlook on life
- supports individuals in aligning with their highest purpose, embracing their inner light, and manifesting their spiritual potential

Zodiac Sign: Leo, Aries, and Taurus

Chakra Alignment: crown

Color(s): most commonly known for their clear or white color, but can also occur in various colors, known as *fancy diamonds*, including red (rarest of all), yellow, blue, pink, and green

Elemental Alignment: fire

Crystal Family: carbon

Crystal Structure: face-centered cubic (FCC) lattice comprises carbon atoms arranged in a repeating pattern of interconnected tetrahedrons

Emerald

Emerald is a precious gemstone that has captivated people for centuries with its vibrant green color and stunning beauty. The history of emerald dates back to ancient times —when it was highly valued by civilizations such as the Egyptians, Greeks, and Romans. It can be found in Colombia, Zambia, Brazil, Afghanistan, and Russia. Cleanse and recharge your emerald by holding it under running, warm water. Never use alcohol on it. It is important to handle emeralds with care as it is a relatively softer gemstone compared to others and can be prone to scratches or damage.

Physical, Emotional, and Spiritual Healing Properties:

- supports the cardiovascular system, enhances vitality, and promotes overall physical well-being
- opens and nurtures the heart, promoting emotional healing, harmony, and unconditional love, and can help attract love, deepen relationships, and foster emotional balance and empathy
- enhances intuition, spiritual insight, and the ability to communicate with higher beings and nature spirits
- supports inner growth, spiritual awakening, and a greater sense of oneness with creation

Zodiac Sign: Gemini, Cancer, Libra, and Taurus

Chakra Alignment: heart

Color(s): vibrant green

Elemental Alignment: earth

Crystal Family: beryl

Crystal Structure: hexagonal

Epidote

Epidote is a beautiful green mineral known for its unique crystalline formations and powerful energetic properties. It exists in metamorphic and igneous rocks and often occurs in combination with other minerals. It can be found in Austria, Norway, the United States, and Madagascar. To cleanse the epidote, hold it under running water for two minutes and pat dry with a soft cloth.

Physical, Emotional, and Spiritual Healing Properties:

- carries energizing and rejuvenating properties
- promotes overall health and vitality
- supports the body's natural healing processes, alleviates fatigue, and strengthens the physical body
- brings clarity, releases negative emotions, and promotes emotional healing
- encourages self-confidence, optimism, and a positive outlook on life
- helps let go of patterns of self-doubt, negativity, and emotional blockages

Zodiac Sign: Gemini

Chakra Alignment: heart and solar plexus

Color(s): green

Elemental Alignment: earth

Crystal Family: silicate

Crystal Structure: can exhibit a variety of crystal formations, including prismatic, tabular, and acicular

Fluorite

Fluorite displays a wide range of vibrant hues. Made of calcium fluoride, it is renowned for its stunning crystal formations and fluorescence under ultraviolet light. Its name derives from the Latin *fluere*, meaning flow. It is used as a flux in metallurgy and can be found in China, Mexico, the United States, and Brazil. To cleanse fluorite, let it bathe in the moonlight overnight.

Physical, Emotional, and Spiritual Healing Properties:

- has cleansing and purifying properties
- supports lung health, alleviates respiratory conditions, and enhances overall physical well-being
- brings balance and clarity to the mind, promoting mental focus, concentration, and decision-making
- helps you let go of negative patterns, reduce anxiety, and enhance emotional resilience

Zodiac Sign: Aquarius

Chakra Alignment: third eye and crown

Color(s): Purple, green, blue, yellow, and pink (some fluorite specimens display multiple colors within a crystal, creating a beautiful and vibrant visual effect).

Elemental Alignment: air

Crystal Family: halides

Crystal Structure: cubic

Fuchsite

Fuchsite is named after Johann Nepomuk von Fuchs, a German chemist and minerologist. It can be found in Brazil, India, Russia, and the United States. Try cleansing this crystal through visualization and meditation. Avoid exposing it to prolonged sunlight so that there's no discoloration.

Physical, Emotional, and Spiritual Healing Properties:

- supports the respiratory system, alleviates allergies, and aids in detoxification
- promotes emotional balance, self-love, and helps release negative emotions
- enhances connection with nature, nurtures spiritual growth, and assists in accessing higher realms of consciousness

Zodiac Sign: Aquarius

Chakra Alignment: heart

Color(s): vibrant green color, often with shimmering metallic flecks

Elemental Alignment: earth

Crystal Family: mica mineral family as a green variety of muscovite, a silicate mineral

Crystal Structure: monoclinic crystal structure, characterized by its layered and platy appearance

Garnet

Commonly found in a lush shade of red, garnet was highly valued in ancient cultures, including Greek, Egyptian, and Roman civilizations. Its name comes from *granatum* (Latin) and can be found in India, Brazil, Sri Lanka, Madagascar, and the United States. They are commonly found in metamorphic rocks and alluvial deposits. To cleanse garnet, you can use methods such as running water, smudging with sage or incense, or placing it on a bed of hematite stones. Avoid exposing garnet to harsh chemicals or prolonged sunlight, as it may cause fading or damage to the crystal's color and energetic properties.

Physical, Emotional, and Spiritual Healing Properties:

- supports the circulatory system and promotes healthy blood flow (May, 2022)
- enhances vitality and energy levels
- assists in reducing inflammation (Navratan, 2022)
- stimulates passion, love, and commitment in relationships
- awakens the kundalini energy and balances the flow of energy throughout the body

Zodiac Sign: Aquarius

Chakra Alignment:

- Almandine: root and heart
- Pyrope: root, heart, and crown
- Spessartine: sacral, solar plexus, and root
- Tsavorite: heart
- Demantoid: heart
- Rhodolite: root, heart, and crown

Color(s): deep red (almandine and pyrope), orange (spessartine), green (tsavorite and demantoid), and purple (rhodolite)

Elemental Alignment:

- Almandine: fire and earth
- Pyrope: fire and earth
- Spessartine: fire and earth
- Tsavorite: water
- Demantoid: water
- Rhodolite: earth, fire, and water

Crystal Family: nesosilicates

Crystal Structure: cubic

Genesis Stone

Genesis stones are beautiful specimens that have been carved by the culminated effect of the wind and age. Each stone is a combination of magnetite, hematite, and jasper.

It can be found in the United States, particularly in Utah. This hardy gemstone may be cleansed by holding it under running water or recharging it in the sunlight for a few hours.

Physical, Emotional, and Spiritual Healing Properties:

- supports the overall well-being of the physical body
- very effective as a worry stone and can dispel negative thoughts and anxiety
- helps banish nightmares

Zodiac Sign: Taurus

Chakra Alignment: root and heart

Color(s): red, brown, and white

Elemental Alignment: earth

Crystal Family: silicate

Crystal Structure: granular or aggregate structure

Hematite

In ancient Egypt, hematite was used for jewelry and as a cosmetic pigment. Native American tribes have also used hematite for spiritual and healing practices. Its name is from the Greek word *haima*, meaning blood, due to its reddish-brown color when powdered. Hematite can be found in Brazil, Australia, China, India, and the United

States. It is commonly found in sedimentary deposits, as well as in metamorphic and igneous rocks. This crystal cannot be cleaned with water, but you can use cleansing crystals, smoke, or rest it on a moonlit windowsill for an entire night.

Physical, Emotional, and Spiritual Healing Properties:

- supports blood circulation and helps in the formation of red blood cells (Healing Energy Rocks, 2021)
- assists in treating anemia and related symptoms
- helps in grounding and connecting with the Earth's energy
- enhances psychic protection and deflects negative energies
- supports the manifestation of one's intentions

Zodiac Sign: Aries

Chakra Alignment: root

Color(s): back, gray, or reddish-brown

Elemental Alignment: earth

Crystal Family: oxide mineral family

Crystal Structure: trigonal crystal structure with rhombohedral or tabular-shaped crystals

Hiddenite

Hiddenite was discovered in the late 19th century by William Earl Hidden, after whom it is named. Hiddenite was first found in Alexander County, North Carolina, USA, and can also be found in Brazil, Madagascar, Afghanistan, and Myanmar. Avoid direct sunlight exposure for prolonged periods with this stone. Try cleansing with sound or smudging.

Physical, Emotional, and Spiritual Healing Properties:

- supports the heart and circulatory system (*Crystal Vaults*, 2023b)
- enhances physical vitality and rejuvenation
- very effective in healing emotional distress in children (*Crystal Vaults*, 2023b)
- stimulates spiritual growth and expansion of consciousness
- promotes a sense of inner peace and spiritual alignment

Zodiac Sign: Libra

Chakra Alignment: heart

Color(s): light to medium green color, ranging from pale green to a vibrant, intense green hue

Elemental Alignment: earth and water

Crystal Family: pyroxene mineral family

Crystal Structure: a monoclinic crystal structure forming prismatic or tabular crystals

Howlite

Howlite was discovered in Nova Scotia, Canada, in the 19th century by Henry How, a Canadian chemist and geologist. It was named after him. Howlite is primarily found in Canada, particularly in Nova Scotia. Other regions where it exists include the United States (California and Nevada), Mexico, Russia, and Germany. Howlite is best cleansed under the moonlight. Avoid contact with water or salt when possible.

Physical, Emotional, and Spiritual Healing Properties:

- aids in calcium absorption and balances calcium levels in the body (Borates Today, 2022)
- assists in relieving muscle tension and cramps
- promotes restful sleep and alleviates insomnia
- enhances patience and reduces anger or irritability
- facilitates the release of emotional attachments

Zodiac Sign: Gemini

Chakra Alignment: crown and third eye

Color(s): naturally occurs in white or colorless form, but is often dyed to resemble other gemstones, such as turquoise or lapis lazuli

Elemental Alignment: earth

Crystal Family: borate

Crystal Structure: a monoclinic crystal structure forming in prismatic or tabular crystals

Iolite

Iolite, also known as Vikings' Compass or water sapphire, has a rich history and has been valued for centuries. The name iolite originates from ios—the Greek word meaning violet. It was first discovered in Norway in the 18th century. Throughout history, iolite has been used as a navigational aid by Vikings and seafarers to determine the sun's position on cloudy days. It can be found in Sri Lanka, India, Brazil, Madagascar, Tanzania, and the United States (Wyoming and Connecticut). Iolite is a soft stone and is best cleansed through sound or moonlight. Avoid exposing it to direct sunlight.

Physical, Emotional, and Spiritual Healing Properties:

- enhances the body's detoxification processes (Abouzelof, 2023)
- assists in reducing migraines and headaches
- enhances self-expression and communication skills
- stimulates intuitive abilities and enhances spiritual insight

Zodiac Sign: Libra

Chakra Alignment: third eye

Color(s): ranges in color from pale blue-violet to deep indigo-blue

Elemental Alignment: water

Crystal Family: cordierite

Crystal Structure: orthorhombic

Jade

Jade holds immense cultural significance in various civilizations, including ancient China, Mesoamerica, and New Zealand. The term jade refers to two different minerals: nephrite and jadeite. Nephrite jade has been used in China for over 5,000 years, while jadeite became popular during the Ming Dynasty. Jade has been revered as a symbol of purity, wisdom, and protection. It can be found in China, Myanmar (Burma), Russia, Guatemala, New Zealand, and the United States (California and Wyoming). Running it under water is the best for cleansing jade.

Physical, Emotional, and Spiritual Healing Properties:

- promotes overall well-being and vitality
- balances body fluids and removes toxins (Cho, 2022b)
- supports healthy skin and hair

- facilitates spiritual growth and insight
- encourages balance and alignment of the mind, body, and spirit

Zodiac Sign:

- Green Jade: Libra, Taurus, Aries, and Gemini
- White Jade: Libra and Pisces
- Lavender Jade: Libra and Taurus
- Yellow Jade: Libra and Virgo
- Black Jade: Libra and Taurus

Chakra Alignment: heart

- Green Jade: heart
- White Jade: heart and crown
- Lavender Jade: heart and crown
- Yellow Jade: solar plexus
- Black Jade: root

Elemental Alignment: earth

Crystal Family: jadeite mineral family (jadeite variety) and the nephrite mineral family (nephrite variety)

Crystal Structure: The crystal structure of jade varies depending on the variety. Nephrite jade has a fibrous or granular structure, while jadeite jade has a microcrystalline interlocking structure.

Jasper

Jasper has been used by civilizations throughout history. It is highly valued for its aesthetic and perceived metaphysical properties. The name comes from the Greek word *iaspis*, which means spotted stone. Jasper has been used for various purposes, including jewelry, amulets, and decorative items. It can be found in Brazil, India, Russia, Australia, Madagascar, and the United States (specifically Oregon, Idaho, and Washington). This crystal can be cleansed under the light of the moon, and it can also be rinsed off. But do not submerge it in water for too long, or it may rust.

Physical, Emotional, and Spiritual Healing Properties:

- supports overall physical vitality and stamina
- enhances circulation and detoxification
- assists in balancing and strengthening the immune system (Anahana, 2023b)
- facilitates connection with the Earth's energy and nature spirits
- enhances spiritual grounding and stability

Zodiac Sign:

- Red Jasper: Aries and Scorpio
- Yellow Jasper: Leo
- Brown Jasper: Capricorn and Cancer
- Green Jasper: Cancer, Aries, and Pisces

Chakra Alignment:

- Red Jasper: root
- Yellow Jasper: root and solar plexus
- Brown Jasper: root
- Green Jasper: root and heart

Color(s): all the colors listed above, but also exist in multi-colored varieties

Elemental Alignment: earth

Crystal Family: quartz

Crystal Structure: cryptocrystalline, forming as fine-grained aggregates or nodules

Kyanite

Kyanite gets its name from the word *kyanos*, which means dark blue in Greek. Kyanite has been appreciated for its unique crystal structure and metaphysical properties. It can be found in Brazil, India, Nepal, Switzerland, Zimbabwe, and the United States. To cleanse, place your kyanite in a bowl full of sea salt for an hour.

Physical, Emotional, and Spiritual Healing Properties:

- assists in the healing of the throat and larynx (Charms of Light, 2023b)
- supports the respiratory system and aids in breathing

- facilitates communication and self-expression
- assists in meditation and accessing higher states of consciousness

Color(s): blue, green, black, and white

Zodiac Sign:

- Blue Kyanite: Aries, Taurus, and Libra
- Green Kyanite: Pisces
- Black Kyanite: Aries, Libra
- White Kyanite: Gemini, Sagittarius, and Pisces

Chakra Alignment:

- Blue Kyanite: throat and third eye
- Green Kyanite: heart
- Black Kyanite: root
- White Kyanite: crown

Elemental Alignment:

- Blue Kyanite: water and air
- Green Kyanite: earth
- Black Kyanite: air
- White Kyanite: all elements

Crystal Family: silicate

Crystal Structure: a triclinic crystal structure, forming in long, flat blade-like crystals or fibrous aggregates

Kunzite

Kunzite is a relatively new gemstone, unearthed in the 20th century. It was named after the renowned gemologist George Frederick Kunz, who identified and popularized the stone. It can be found in Brazil, Afghanistan, Pakistan, the United States (specifically California), Madagascar, and Myanmar. Warm, soapy water is best for cleansing kunzite.

Physical, Emotional, and Spiritual Healing Properties:

- supports the cardiovascular system and blood circulation (Chee, 2021a)
- assists in hormonal balance and alleviates menstrual discomfort (Chee, 2021a)
- promotes overall vitality and energy flow in the body
- aids in recovery from physical exhaustion or illness
- supports the journey of self-discovery and spiritual awakening

Zodiac Sign: Taurus

Chakra Alignment: heart and third eye

Color(s): pink, lilac

Elemental Alignment: water

Crystal Family: spodumene family

Crystal Structure: monoclinic

Labradorite

Labradorite is named after the Labrador Peninsula in Canada, where it was discovered in the late 18th century. It has been known to indigenous cultures for centuries and holds mystical and spiritual significance in various traditions. It can be found in Canada, Madagascar, Finland, Russia, and the United States. Labradorite does well when cleansed and charged under the moonlight.

Physical, Emotional, and Spiritual Healing Properties:

- assists in relieving symptoms of colds, bronchitis, and allergies (*Labradorite Healing Properties*, 2023)
- helps in balancing hormones and regulating metabolism
- enhances physical stamina and vitality
- enhances intuition and psychic abilities
- encourages perseverance and determination in pursuing goals

Zodiac Sign: Leo and Scorpio

Chakra Alignment: third eye and crown

Color(s): displays a unique play of colors known as labradorescence and exhibits iridescent flashes of blue, green, yellow, and purple when viewed from different angles

Elemental Alignment: water and earth

Crystal Family: feldspar family

Crystal Structure: triclinic

Lapis Lazuli

Lapis lazuli has a rich history dating back thousands of years. It has been highly prized by ancient civilizations, including the Egyptians, Sumerians, and Persians, and was revered for its deep blue color and association with royalty and spirituality. It can be found in Afghanistan, Chile, Russia, and the United States (specifically Colorado and California). It can be cleansed alongside other gemstones, such as clear quartz, but refrain from using water with raw lapis lazuli as this may cause unwanted chemical reactions.

Physical, Emotional, and Spiritual Healing Properties:

- assists in relieving headaches and migraines (Camille, 2021)
- enhances vitality and boosts energy levels
- helps with insomnia and promotes restful sleep
- aids in accessing and understanding past lives

Zodiac Sign: Sagittarius and Libra

Chakra Alignment: third eye and throat

Color(s): deep blue color, often with golden flecks of pyrite and white veins of calcite

Elemental Alignment: water and air

Crystal Family: feldspar

Crystal Structure: amorphous

Larimar

Larimar was discovered in the 20th century in the Dominican Republic. It is often associated with the Caribbean and is sometimes called the Atlantis Stone due to legends linking it to the lost city of Atlantis. It can be found in Barahona and can be cleansed by using a soft-bristled brush to remove dust from the surface, and then by washing it with warm, soapy water.

Physical, Emotional, and Spiritual Healing Properties:

- soothes the nervous system and promotes relaxation (Crystals & Holistic Healing, n.d.)
- supports the throat and respiratory system
- helps with pain relief and inflammation
- assists in connecting with the divine feminine energy

Zodiac Sign: Leo

Chakra Alignment: throat and heart

Color(s): soft blue color, ranging from light turquoise to deep blue-green

Elemental Alignment: water

Crystal Family: pectolite

Crystal Structure: triclinic

Malachite

Malachite has been used for various purposes over many years, including jewelry, decorative objects, and pigments. It was highly valued by ancient civilizations such as the Egyptians, Greeks, and Romans. It can be found in Russia, the Democratic Republic of Congo, Zambia, Australia, and the United States. Try leaving malachite on a windowsill under the moonlight to cleanse and recharge it.

Physical, Emotional, and Spiritual Healing Properties:

- supports recovery from asthma, intestinal issues, and rheumatic discomfort (Gem Pundit, 2022)
- promotes overall physical well-being and vitality
- enhances emotional healing and stability
- encourages positive transformation and personal growth
- promotes connection with nature and earth energies

Zodiac Sign: Scorpio and Capricorn

Chakra Alignment: heart and solar plexus

Color(s): vibrant green

Elemental Alignment: earth

Crystal Family: carbonate

Crystal Structure: monoclinic

Merlinite

Merlinite, also known as Dendritic Opal or Dendritic Agate, is a relatively recent discovery. It can be found in New Mexico, the USA, Australia, Brazil, and Madagascar. Cleanse your stone with warm water and mild soap.

Physical, Emotional, and Spiritual Healing Properties:

- aids in recovery from chronic fatigue, migraines, aches, and pains (Abouzelof, 2018)
- can help release tensions associated with endometriosis (Abouzelof, 2018)
- enhances emotional balance and stability
- encourages acceptance and adaptation to change
- supports spiritual exploration and expansion

Zodiac Sign: Gemini

Chakra Alignment: third eye and crown

Color(s): black or gray in color, often with white or gray dendritic inclusions that resemble tree branches or fern-like patterns

Elemental Alignment: earth and water

Crystal Family: quartz

Crystal Structure: cryptocrystalline

Moldavite

Moldavite is a rare gemstone formed from the impact of a meteor crash around 15 million years ago in the current Czech Republic. It is highly regarded for its metaphysical properties and can be found in the southern region of the Czech Republic, near the Moldau River (Vltava River). Small quantities have also been found in Germany and Austria. Cleanse moldavite by recharging it under moonlight overnight.

Physical, Emotional, and Spiritual Healing Properties:

- supports physical transformation and regeneration
- relieves gastrointestinal problems (Tiny Rituals, 2023c)
- encourages emotional balance and clarity
- heals emotional and mental wounds

Zodiac Sign: Scorpio, Taurus, and Aquarius

Chakra Alignment: heart and third eye

Color(s): pale green to deep forest green

Elemental Alignment: air

Crystal Family: tektite

Crystal Structure: amorphous

Moonstone

Moonstone has a rich history and has been revered in various cultures for centuries. It holds divine lunar energy and is considered a sacred stone in many traditions. It can be found in Sri Lanka, India, Myanmar (Burma), Australia, and the United States. Leaving this stone under the moonlight is the best way to cleanse your moonstones.

Physical, Emotional, and Spiritual Healing Properties:

- supports hormonal balance and reproductive health (Nast, 2020)
- promotes healthy digestion and soothes digestive issues
- encourages emotional openness and receptivity
- facilitates connection with the divine feminine and lunar energies

Zodiac Sign: Cancer, Libra, and Scorpio

Chakra Alignment: third eye and crown

Color(s): white, cream, peach, gray, and blue

Elemental Alignment: water

Crystal Family: feldspar

Crystal Structure: monoclinic

Nuummite

Nuummite is a rare and ancient stone (also known as the *Sorcerer's Stone*) that is found primarily in Greenland. It is among the oldest minerals and holds great significance in Inuit culture. It has been used for spiritual and healing purposes for centuries and is found exclusively in the region of Nuuk, Greenland. The safest way to cleanse this crystal is through smudging.

Physical, Emotional, and Spiritual Healing Properties:

- supports physical vitality and strength
- aids in the healing of injuries and wounds
- promotes connection with ancient wisdom and ancestral energies (Crystal Rock Star, 2017)

Zodiac Sign: Scorpio

Chakra Alignment: root and third eye

Color(s): dark, charcoal-black color with shimmering iridescent flashes of gold, bronze, or silver

Elemental Alignment: earth

Crystal Family: amphibole

Crystal Structure: Characterized by layers of tightly packed silicate minerals. Its unique structure contributes to its mesmerizing chatoyancy (cat's eye effect) and iridescence.

Obsidian

Obsidian has a long history and is associated with various ancient civilizations. It has been widely used in tools, weapons, and spiritual practices (Galo, 2023). Obsidian gets its name from Obsius, a Roman explorer who discovered the stone in Ethiopia. It can be found in Mexico, the United States, Iceland, Japan, and Armenia. Warm water and mild soap work best for cleansing this crystal. Avoid leaving it in sunlight or water for too long, as it can make the stone brittle.

Physical, Emotional, and Spiritual Healing Properties:

- aids in pain relief and muscle relaxation (Le Comptoir Geologiqe, n.d.)
- enhances physical endurance and vitality
- enhances self-control and emotional strength
- facilitates grounding and connection with the Earth

Zodiac Sign: Scorpio

Chakra Alignment: root

Color(s): black, brown, gray, and sometimes green or red

Elemental Alignment: earth

Crystal Family: Not classified as a crystal but rather a natural glass. It is formed from volcanic activity and does not possess a crystalline structure.

Onyx

Onyx's name comes from the Greek word onyx, which means claw. Onyx has been valued in various cultures throughout time. It can be found in Brazil, India, Uruguay, and the United States. Use visualization and meditation to cleanse the onyx.

Physical, Emotional, and Spiritual Healing Properties:

- supports strength and stamina
- promotes healthy bones, teeth, and nails (Davis, 2022)
- enhances self-control and decision-making
- promotes protection and warding off negative energies

Zodiac Sign: Leo

Chakra Alignment: root and solar plexus

Color(s): black, brown, gray, and white

Elemental Alignment: earth

Crystal Family: chalcedony

Crystal Structure: trigonal

Opal

Opal's name derives from the Sanskrit word *upala,* which means precious stone. Opals have been valued in various cultures, including ancient civilizations like the Romans and Greeks. It can be found in Australia, Mexico, Brazil, Ethiopia, and the United States. Opal is a relatively soft gemstone and should be handled with care to avoid causing any potential damage. It is best to cleanse opal using gentle methods such as running water and a soft cloth.

Physical, Emotional, and Spiritual Healing Properties:

- assists in regulating the body's water balance (Tiny Rituals, 2023d)
- aids in the healing of skin conditions and infections
- enhances creativity and inspiration
- connects with higher realms and spiritual guides

Zodiac Sign:

- White Opal: Libra
- Black Opal: Libra
- Blue Opal: Cancer
- Green Opal: Cancer

- Pink Opal: Libra
- Yellow Opal: Sagittarius

Chakra Alignment:

- White Opal: crown
- Black Opal: crown and root
- Blue Opal: throat
- Green Opal: heart
- Pink Opal: heart
- Yellow Opal: solar plexus

Elemental Alignment: water and earth

Crystal Family: silicate

Crystal Structure: amorphous

Peridot

Peridot is treasured for its vibrant green color and is considered one of the first gemstones used in jewelry. It can be found in Egypt, Myanmar, Pakistan, China, and the United States. Peridot can be cleansed under moonlight or in the presence of vibrant plants, but it is a delicate stone and cannot handle abrasiveness or high temperatures.

Physical, Emotional, and Spiritual Healing Properties:

- assists in digestion and metabolism
- enhances eye health and vision (Sipos, 2023)
- boosts self-confidence and self-worth
- supports manifestation and abundance

Zodiac Sign: Leo

Chakra Alignment: solar plexus and heart

Color(s): vibrant green

Elemental Alignment: earth

Crystal Family: olivine

Crystal Structure: orthorhombic

Pyrite

Pyrite, also known as Fool's Gold, has a fascinating history and has been used by ancient civilizations for various purposes. Its name is from the Greek word *pyr*, meaning fire. It can be found in Spain, Peru, Russia, China, and the United States (particularly Illinois and Colorado). To cleanse pyrite, you can place it on a bed of hematite or clear quartz crystals overnight. This stone is a brittle one, so avoid submerging it in water, or it will rust.

Physical, Emotional, and Spiritual Healing Properties:

- enhances physical stamina and vitality
- helps strengthen the immune system (Reiki Crystal Products, 2022)
- encourages positive thinking and manifestation
- shields against negative energies and psychic attacks
- promotes a sense of personal power and self-discipline

Zodiac Sign: Leo

Chakra Alignment: solar plexus and root

Color(s): metallic golden color with a brassy luster

Elemental Alignment: fire

Crystal Family: sulfide

Crystal Structure: cubic

Quartz

Quartz is among the most prolific minerals on Earth and has a rich history dating back thousands of years. It is valued for its beauty and metaphysical properties. The name comes from the Slavic word *kwardy*, which means hard. It can be found in Brazil, Madagascar, the United States, and Russia. To cleanse quartz crystals, you can use various methods such as gently rinsing them with water, placing them in moonlight, smudging them with sage or other purifying herbs, and burying them in the Earth for a period of time.

Physical, Emotional, and Spiritual Healing Properties:

- enhances overall vitality and energy levels
- assists in balancing and harmonizing the body (Ress, n.d.)
- amplifies the properties of other crystals and gemstones
- helps with energy cleansing and purification

Zodiac Sign:

- Spirit Quartz: all zodiac signs
- Clear Quartz: all zodiac signs
- Rose Quartz: Taurus and Libra
- Smoky Quartz: Capricorn and Sagittarius

Chakra Alignment:

- Spirit Quartz: all chakras, particularly crown
- Clear Quartz: all chakras, but primarily crown
- Rose Quartz: heart
- Smoky Quartz: root and solar plexus

Color(s):

- Spirit Quartz: purple, white, and yellow
- Clear Quartz: transparent
- Rose Quartz: pale to rich pink
- Smoky Quartz: brown to black

Elemental Alignment:

- Spirit Quartz: air and earth
- Clear Quartz: all elements
- Rose Quartz: water and earth
- Smoky Quartz: earth

Crystal Family: silicate

Crystal Structure: hexagonal

Rhodonite

Rhodonite is a manganese silicate mineral that has been used as a gemstone and ornamental material for centuries. It was discovered in the 19th century in the Ural Mountains of Russia and derives its name from the Greek word *rhodon*, which means rose, due to its pink color. It can be found in Russia, Sweden, Australia, Brazil, and the United States. Cleanse this stone with smudging or breathwork. If you use water, do not submerge it for too long, or it can damage the crystal.

Physical, Emotional, and Spiritual Healing Properties:

- assists in detoxification and purification of the body (Springsteen, n.d.)
- balances the hormones and promotes overall well-being
- encourages forgiveness, compassion, and self-love
- supports meditation and deepens spiritual practices

Zodiac Sign: Taurus

Chakra Alignment: heart, root, and solar plexus

Color(s): pink to reddish-brown with black or gray veining

Elemental Alignment: earth

Crystal Family: silicate mineral family

Crystal Structure: trigonal

Rhodochrosite

Rhodochrosite was first discovered in Romania and later found in other locations worldwide. It can be found in Argentina, Peru, South Africa, and the United States. The best way to cleanse this crystal is under moonlight or by keeping it near a selenite stone.

Physical, Emotional, and Spiritual Healing Properties:

- assists in regulating blood pressure and circulation (HealCrystal, 2023)
- stimulates metabolism and aids in digestion
- promotes self-love, self-acceptance, and self-worth
- stimulates the heart chakra and fosters love and compassion

Zodiac Sign: Leo

Chakra Alignment: heart and solar plexus

Color(s): pale pink to deep red

Elemental Alignment: fire

Crystal Family: carbonate

Crystal Structure: trigonal

Rosasite

Rosasite is a subordinate mineral that forms in the oxidation zones of copper-zinc ore deposits. It can be found in the United States, Mexico, Australia, and Germany. Use a soft cloth or brush to keep your stone physically clean, and cleanse it by smudging.

Physical, Emotional, and Spiritual Healing Properties:

- helps in soothing the mind and creates a sense of mental balance (Crystal Vaults, 2023c)
- encourages compassion, forgiveness, and understanding
- promotes inner peace and serenity

Zodiac Sign: Cancer

Chakra Alignment: throat and heart

Color(s): light blue to greenish-blue, often with a rosy pink tint

Elemental Alignment: water

Crystal Family: carbonate

Crystal Structure: monoclinic

Ruby

Ruby is believed to have originated in regions such as Myanmar (Burma), Sri Lanka (Ceylon), and Thailand. Rubies have been treasured by various cultures, including the ancient Greeks and Romans, as symbols of power, passion, and protection. Aside from the countries listed above, it can also be found in India and Tanzania. Warm, soapy water is the best for cleansing ruby.

Physical, Emotional, and Spiritual Healing Properties:

- boosts vitality and energy levels
- enhances blood circulation (Brahma Gems, 2023)
- stimulates the heart and ignites love
- encourages connection with the divine

Zodiac Sign: Leo

Chakra Alignment: root and heart

Color(s): vibrant red color, ranging from pinkish-red to deep crimson

Elemental Alignment: fire

Crystal Family: corundum

Crystal Structure: hexagonal

Sapphire

Sapphire is associated with royalty and was cherished by ancient civilizations, which include the Greeks and Romans, who believed that sapphires had protective powers. It can be found in Myanmar (Burma), Sri Lanka (Ceylon), Thailand, India, Madagascar, Australia, and the United States. A soft-bristled brush, mild soap, and room-temperature water work best when cleaning this crystal.

Physical, Emotional, and Spiritual Healing Properties:

- promotes healthy metabolism and digestion (Supriya, 2022)
- assists in relieving headaches and migraines
- stimulates mental clarity and focus
- assists in meditation

Zodiac Sign:

- Blue Sapphire: Libra
- Yellow Sapphire: Taurus
- Pink Sapphire: Libra
- Orange Sapphire: Taurus
- Green Sapphire: Taurus

Chakra Alignment: third eye and throat

- Blue Sapphire: throat and third eye
- Yellow Sapphire: solar plexus
- Pink Sapphire: heart
- Orange Sapphire: sacral
- Green Sapphire: heart

Elemental Alignment: water

Crystal Family: corundum

Crystal Structure: hexagonal

Selenite

Selenite derives its name from the Greek word *selene*, meaning moon, due to its moon-like glow. Selenite has been associated with the ancient Greek moon goddess Selene, who was believed to bring divine light and wisdom. It can be found in Mexico, the United States, Morocco, Russia, Greece, and Australia. This delicate crystal should not be placed in water, even for a brief moment, because it is soft and can break away with even the smallest amount of exposure. Selenite can be cleansed with sunlight but shouldn't be exposed for more than a few hours as it can fade. Try cleansing this stone by holding it under smoke from smudging with incense or sage for a minute.

Physical, Emotional, and Spiritual Healing Properties:

- supports skeletal health and bone strength (Healing Crystals, 2010)
- assists in pain relief and reducing inflammation
- enhances emotional healing and forgiveness
- can be used to recharge other stones
- enhances meditation and spiritual practice

Zodiac Sign: Taurus

Chakra Alignment: crown and third eye

Color(s): colorless or translucent

Elemental Alignment: air

Crystal Family: gypsum

Crystal Structure: tabular or prismatic

Sodalite

Sodalite was first discovered in Greenland in the early 19th century. It was later named sodalite due to its sodium content and can be found in Canada, Brazil, Russia, Namibia, and India. Sodalite can be cleansed under running water, but don't submerge it, or it will break. It can also be cleansed by moonlight, but using sunlight can cause it to fade.

Physical, Emotional, and Spiritual Healing Properties:

- supports the immune system and overall health
- enhances metabolism and digestion (Times of India, 2019)
- stimulates clarity of thought and rational thinking
- promotes a sense of inner peace and spiritual alignment

Zodiac Sign: Sagittarius

Chakra Alignment: throat

Color(s): blue, ranging from deep blue to lighter blue with white streaks or patches

Elemental Alignment: water

Crystal Family: feldspar

Crystal Structure: cubic

Sugilite

Sugilite was discovered in 1944 by Ken-ichi Sugi in Japan. It was named after him and has since become a popular and sought-after gemstone. It can be found in South Africa, Japan, Canada, and India. Try utilizing visualization and meditation or breathwork to cleanse it.

Physical, Emotional, and Spiritual Healing Properties:

- calms the nervous system and is great for gentle dreams (Tiny Rituals, 2023e)
- assists in releasing stress and anxiety
- facilitates spiritual growth and awareness

Zodiac Sign: Virgo

Chakra Alignment: third eye and crown

Color(s): purple, ranging from pale lavender to deep violet

Elemental Alignment: water

Crystal Family: cyclosilicate

Crystal Structure: hexagonal

Sunstone

Sunstone was highly valued by the ancient Greeks and Vikings, who associated it with the sun and its life-giving energy. Sunstone was also believed to bring abundance, vitality, and good luck. It can be found in India, Norway, Canada, Russia, and the United States. Warm water and mild soap will cleanse your sunstone.

Physical, Emotional, and Spiritual Healing Properties:

- assists in regulating digestion and metabolism
- helps alleviate seasonal affective disorder (SAD) (Oakes, n.d.)
- stimulates joy, warmth, and positivity
- promotes spiritual growth and manifestation

Zodiac Sign: Leo

Chakra Alignment: sacral and solar plexus

Color(s): orange, red, brown, and gold

Elemental Alignment: fire

Crystal Family: feldspar

Crystal Structure: triclinic

Tanzanite

Tanzanite was discovered in 1967. It quickly gained popularity due to its striking blue-violet color and unique optical properties. It can be found in the Merelani Hills of northern Tanzania. To cleanse tanzanite, keep it near selenite or place it on a selenite charging plate.

Physical, Emotional, and Spiritual Healing Properties:

- assists in healing the throat and lungs (Caryl, 2023)
- helps recover from skin issues (Caryl, 2023)
- facilitates emotional healing and trauma resolution------
- enhances feelings of compassion and empathy
- assists in aligning with one's life purpose and spiritual growth

Zodiac Sign: Sagittarius

Chakra Alignment: third eye and crown

Color(s): blue-violet hues

Elemental Alignment: air

Crystal Family: zoisite

Crystal Structure: monoclinic

Tiger's Eye

Tiger's Eye is a popular gemstone known for its unique chatoyancy, which creates a mesmerizing optical effect resembling the eye of a tiger. It can be found in South Africa, Australia, India, and the United States. To cleanse Tiger's Eye, try placing it on a bed of rice overnight. Avoid exposing raw Tiger's Eye to water because it can be toxic.

Physical, Emotional, and Spiritual Healing Properties:

- aids in relieving chronic pain and reducing inflammation (Springsteen, 2023)
- enhances willpower and self-discipline
- assists in manifesting one's intentions and goals

Zodiac Sign: Leo

Chakra Alignment: solar plexus and third eye

Color(s): golden to brownish hues with bands of iridescent chatoyancy

Elemental Alignment: fire

Crystal Family: quartz

Crystal Structure: fibrous crystal structure

Topaz

Topaz has been used for its beauty and healing properties. The name *topaz* comes from the Greek word *topazion*, which refers to a yellow gemstone that was mined on the island of Topazos in the Red Sea. It can be found in Brazil, Russia, Sri Lanka, Nigeria, and the United States. Warm, soapy water will cleanse your lovely topaz crystal.

Physical, Emotional, and Spiritual Properties:

- assists in relieving tension and headaches (Cho, 2022a)
- encourages feelings of joy, confidence, and self-worth
- helps connect with higher realms and spiritual guides

Zodiac Sign:

- White/Colorless Topaz: Sagittarius
- Yellow/Golden Topaz: Leo and Scorpio
- Blue Topaz: Sagittarius
- Pink Topaz: Sagittarius and Scorpio

Chakra Alignment:

- White/Colorless Topaz: crown
- Yellow/Golden Topaz: solar plexus and sacral
- Blue Topaz: throat and third eye

- Pink Topaz: heart

Elemental Alignment:

- White/Colorless Topaz: fire
- Yellow/Golden Topaz: earth and fire
- Blue Topaz: water, air, and fire
- Pink Topaz: fire

Crystal Family: silicate

Crystal Structure: orthorhombic

Tourmaline

Dutch traders first documented tourmaline in the late 1600s and brought the gemstone from Sri Lanka to Europe, where it gained popularity. The name comes from *turmali,* in Sinhalese. It means mixed gemstones. Tourmaline can be found in Sri Lanka, Brazil, Afghanistan, Nigeria, and the United States. To cleanse, gently hold it under lukewarm running water.

Physical, Emotional, and Spiritual Healing Properties:

- assists in balancing the nervous system (Young, 2021)
- supports detoxification and elimination of toxins
- encourages compassion and understanding
- promotes a sense of protection and energetic cleansing

Zodiac Sign:

- Black Tourmaline: Libra, Scorpio, Capricorn
- Green Tourmaline: Capricorn
- Pink Tourmaline: Libra
- Blue Tourmaline: Libra and Taurus
- Watermelon Tourmaline: Gemini and Virgo

Chakra Alignment:

- Black Tourmaline: root
- Green Tourmaline: heart
- Pink Tourmaline: heart
- Blue Tourmaline: throat and third eye
- Watermelon Tourmaline: heart

Elemental Alignment:

- Black Tourmaline: earth and water
- Green Tourmaline: earth
- Pink Tourmaline: water
- Blue Tourmaline: water
- Watermelon Tourmaline: water

Crystal Family: silicate

Crystal Structure: prismatic crystals with vertical striations

Turquoise

Turquoise has a rich history that dates back thousands of years. It has been highly prized by ancient civilizations such as the Egyptians, Native Americans, and Persians. The name comes from the French term *pierre turquoise*, meaning Turkish stone, as it was originally brought to Europe from Turkey and can be found in Iran, Afghanistan, China, Mexico, and the United States. Turquoise does well with smoke cleansing but should avoid water because it may be subject to chemical reactions, fading, and cracking. We also shouldn't leave turquoise under the sunlight for too long because it can cause the brilliant colors to fade.

Physical, Emotional, and Spiritual Healing Properties:

- supports overall physical well-being and vitality
- supports the healing of various issues related to the stomach, including acidity (Charms of Light, 2023c)
- brings a sense of joy, serenity, and positive energy
- supports spiritual growth and self-discovery

Zodiac Sign: Sagittarius, Pisces, and Scorpio

Chakra Alignment: throat

Color(s): vibrant blues and greens

Elemental Alignment: earth and water

Crystal Family: phosphate

Crystal Structure: triclinic

Unakite

Unakite is a relatively recent discovery, first identified in the Unaka Range of North Carolina, USA, from which it derives its name. It was named by a geologist named Richard Jahns in the early 20th century and can be found in the United States, South Africa, Brazil, China, and Zimbabwe. Cleanse unakite through sound or under the moonlight.

Physical, Emotional, and Spiritual Healing Properties:

- helps with healthy hair and nails (Chee, 2021b)
- promotes emotional healing and release of old patterns
- fosters a sense of inner peace and connection
- assists in aligning with one's higher purpose

Zodiac Sign: Scorpio

Chakra Alignment: heart

Color(s): green and pink

Elemental Alignment: earth and water

Crystal Family: granite

Crystal Structure: monoclinic

Vanadinite

Vanadinite is a mineral that was first discovered in the 19th century in the Zimapán region of Mexico. Its name is derived from the element vanadium, which is present in its chemical composition. It can be found in the United States, especially in Arizona and New Mexico. Try cleansing vanadinite with sound.

Physical, Emotional, and Spiritual Healing Properties:

- assists in relieving breathing problems (Healing with Crystals, n.d.)
- assists in overcoming procrastination and lethargy
- supports grounding and connection to the Earth
- promotes balance and harmony between the physical and spiritual realms

Zodiac Sign: Capricorn

Chakra Alignment: root and sacral

Color(s): red, orange, brown, and yellow

Elemental Alignment: fire and earth

Crystal Family: apatite

Crystal Structure: hexagonal

Zircon

Zircon was used in various ancient cultures, including those in India, Persia, and Greece. Zircon comes from the Persian word zargun, meaning gold-colored. It can be found in Australia, Brazil, Sri Lanka, Thailand, and the United States. Try cleansing zircon in the presence of cleansing stones such as clear quartz.

Physical, Emotional, and Spiritual Healing Properties:

- supports the health of the reproductive system (Rudraksha Ratna, n.d.)
- promotes inner peace and harmony
- facilitates spiritual growth and transformation

Zodiac Sign: Sagittarius

Chakra Alignment: root, sacral, and solar plexus

Color(s): yellow, orange, brown, and blue

Elemental Alignment: earth and water

Crystal Family: nesosilicate

Crystal Structure: tetragonal

Whew! So, in this chapter, we went through the profiles of some of the most beautifully prolific crystals that can help enhance your manifestations. Now that you know about different crystals, the next vital question is: What do you choose for your grid? We will cover more on this in the next chapter.

CHAPTER 8

CHOOSING THE RIGHT CRYSTAL FOR THE JOB

Now that we've learned about different crystals, you may be wondering—what will suit my needs best? This chapter goes over suggestions for center stones and discusses the outcomes you can expect from different types. You will also learn how to select stones utilizing signs, your intuition, and the tenets of ethical sourcing.

SPIRITUAL ENHANCEMENT

Agate, Aventurine, Calcite, Fluorite, Howlite, Carnelian, Kyanite

Crystals hold a profound ability to assist in our spiritual enhancement. In a chaotic world, seeking solace, connection, and a deeper understanding of our inner selves is natural. Crystals offer a gentle yet powerful support system that resonates with our energy and guides us spiritually.

Through their unique vibrations, crystals help to align our chakras, clear energy blockages, and raise our spiritual consciousness. They act as catalysts, amplifying our intentions and providing a tangible focus for our spiritual practices. Crystals can bring clarity, promote mindfulness, and awaken our intuitive abilities, fostering a sense of inner peace and balance (Rekstis, 2018).

We deepen the connection with their energy by incorporating crystals as center stones in our spiritual practices. Select a crystal based on your intention and place it in a sacred space or carry it throughout the day. Meditate with the crystal, holding it in your hand or putting it on your body, allowing its energy to permeate your being. Trust your intuition to guide you in utilizing crystals for spiritual enhancement, and embrace the transformative journey they offer with open hearts and minds.

PROSPERITY AND ABUNDANCE

Pyrite, Citrine, Emerald, Green Jade, Green Aventurine, Moss Agate

Crystals hold the potential to enhance prosperity and abundance, guiding us toward a more bountiful existence. They work holistically to transform our mindset, amplify intentions, and clear blockages. Crystals like citrine, pyrite, and green aventurine help shift limiting beliefs, fostering self-confidence and a positive outlook on life.

Through their unique vibrational qualities, crystals serve as powerful allies in attracting and manifesting abundance. By infusing them with our intentions, we create a potent, energetic resonance that magnetizes opportunities and aligns us with the flow of prosperity (Truly Experiences Blog, 2021).

Certain crystals, such as clear quartz and citrine, also aid in clearing energetic blockages, releasing fears and a scarcity mindset, and allowing abundant energy to flow freely into our lives. To utilize abundance crystals as center stones in crystal grids, select a focal crystal that resonates with your intention for abundance first.

EMOTIONAL HEALING

Amethyst, Rose Quartz, Moonstone, Obsidian, Clear Quartz, Blue Lace Agate

Emotional healing is vital as it allows us to acknowledge, process, and release emotional wounds, leading to personal growth, inner peace, and overall well-being. Unresolved emotions can create blockages, impacting our mental, emotional, and physical health. Crystals are powerful allies in this healing journey by offering support and energetic alignment.

Crystals' unique vibrations resonate with our emotional energy centers, restoring balance and harmony. Stones, like rose quartz and amethyst, are renowned for promoting emotional healing (Pacinello, 2011). Rose quartz, the stone of compassion, nurtures self-love and heals emotional trauma. Amethyst assists in releasing negative emotions and promotes mental clarity. Blue lace agate soothes and calms the mind, facilitating effective communication and healing emotional wounds.

To use a center stone for emotional healing in a crystal grid, select a crystal that resonates with your intention, such as rose quartz. Surround it with supportive crystals like amethyst and blue lace agate.

PHYSICAL HEALING

Citrine, Moonstone, Tiger's Eye, Lapis Lazuli,
Bloodstone, Turquoise

It is normal to get exhausted with the grind of daily life and experience the urge for some respite. Physical healing is essential for our overall well-being, and crystals can support this process. For example, citrine enhances vitality and stimulates the body's natural healing abilities. It boosts energy levels, helps with digestion, and promotes overall physical wellness.

Bloodstone is another powerful healing stone that is associated with purifying the blood and detoxifying the body.

Bloodstone also alleviates physical ailments and promotes physical strength and endurance. Tiger's Eye supports the body's natural healing process, especially in fatigue or chronic illnesses. Tiger's Eye enhances physical strength, promotes balance and stability, and increases vitality.

To incorporate these stones into a crystal grid for physical healing, choose one as a center stone and surround it with supportive crystals. Place citrine, bloodstone, or Tiger's Eye at the center and complement it with other crystals known for their physical healing properties.

The kind of crystal you choose will always depend on the type of healing you want to achieve. However, at the onset, it's normal to be overwhelmed simply because there are so many options. For all my beginner witches, here is a **starter kit** containing the best, friendliest crystals for your grid. This kit comprises agate, amber, amethyst, bloodstone, citrine, emerald, hematite, jade, jasper, malachite, moonstone, obsidian, spirit quartz, clear quartz, rose quartz, selenite, Tiger's Eye, and black tourmaline.

BONUS: 6 INTENSE AND POWERFUL CRYSTALS AND STONES

For those of you who'd like to go even deeper, here are some bonus stones that aren't as common. These are known to be powerful, so if you're interested or if they're available to you, definitely consider adding them to your grid!

Moqui Marbles

Also known as Shaman Stones, these beautiful crystals can be sourced from southern Utah. The Hopi Indian shamans revere moqui marbles and often use them in ritual practices. The healing properties of this crystal include:

- grounding and centering
- balancing your energies
- connecting you to the core energy of nature and Mother Earth
- stimulating psychic capacities
- helping you access higher knowledge
- healing the root chakra

Auralite-23

Auralite-23 radiates divine energy and is excellent for those who love meditating. The common name for this is *red cap amethyst.* The stone is ancient and rare and was first formed over a billion years ago. The "23" refers to the number of minerals in the stone, although the average auralite usually has fewer minerals.

Scientists believe this variant formed when meteorites struck the Earth. A little Aurelite-23 can contain silver, magnetite, platinum, epidote, copper, gialite, and many more minerals. The stone was only discovered in 2007 and can only be found to the north of Lake Superior in

Ontario, Canada. The benefits of the stone include the following:

- helps enter deeply meditative states
- increases awareness
- enhances mental stamina
- heals and balances our bodies
- balances the solar plexus chakra

Astrophyllite

Rare and highly sought-after, astrophyllite comes from the Greek words *astron* ("star") and *phyllon* ("leaf"). It is usually opaque to translucent and has star-like patterns. It has a high-vibrational energy and is only found in a few places like Russia, Norway, Canada, and Greenland. Its benefits include the following:

- heightening perception
- deepening our relationships
- healing emotional traumas
- balancing the crown chakra
- harmonizing the heart and sacral chakras

Since this stone is particularly aesthetic, it's featured in jewelry, and this can be the best way to infuse your spirit with its vibrational energies.

Shungite

Rich black and very rare, shungite is a miracle stone that only exists in Russia. It is a marriage of carbon and graphite, and because of its unique *fullerenes* (it contains carbon in spherical ions), it can absorb harmful ultraviolet radiations and keep you safe. The healing properties of shungite include the following:

- grounding and stabilizing your energies
- protecting against harmful radiation
- improving mental focus
- balancing and amplifying your root chakra
- harboring spiritual transformation

Seraphinite

This beautiful crystal is also among the strongest, and its energy is so intense you can feel it as soon as you touch it! It is a stone for spiritual enlightenment. Its name is inspired by one of the highest angel orders, the Seraphims. This is the stone for you if you're seeking high vibrational energies. Among other things, it helps you to:

- find balance
- cleanse and heal all chakras
- experience accelerated spiritual growth
- connect with divine spirits
- cleanse your nervous system
- become more aware

- live from the heart

With its enchanting green hues and chatoyancy effect, seraphinite is one of the most beautiful crystals out there. But it isn't something you'll find in conventional chain jewelry stores. The look of each gemstone is unique, and its patterns vary between gems. The stone is also soft, so it's not for daily wear. But independent shops can feature it, and you can also keep the stone for your gridwork, particularly if you're seeking an entire chakra cleansing.

Impactite

The origins of this crystal go back 500 million years when a meteorite struck the Earth's surface. This crystal exists in Norway and bears intense energy. Using this stone with moldavite can amplify the powers of both crystals, so much so that all negative energies may experience complete and total flushing. However, the powers of both stones are intense, so I suggest that you wait and familiarize yourself with grid craft before trying to work with anything this advanced. The benefits of impactite include:

- clearing energy blockages
- increasing awareness
- awakening self-healing
- protecting auras
- dispelling negative energies
- generating abundance

Impactite will bring a state of higher consciousness and greater awareness to your meditative practices.

OTHER FACTORS TO CONSIDER FOR CRYSTAL SELECTION

Signs From the Universe

Now that you've gotten a fair idea of what crystals you can use for your gridwork, it's time to get into some procedural nitty-gritty. The first of these is my favorite, and it is all about opening your heart to the signs of the universe. When thinking, praying, or meditating, look inside and speak to the world around you. Ask the energies surrounding you to send you a sign, and you'll be surprised at the secrets you unlock. A long time back, I was on the brink of a very difficult decision. It involved letting go of someone I loved dearly but whose energy had become parasitic. When I prayed to the universe for a sign, here's what I learned. No matter your thoughts or feelings, when something isn't serving your purpose, life itself will come together in multiple ways to *show you that you need to let go.* It'll keep showing you again and again—but we often close our eyes, shut our doors, and refuse to let change happen. The first thing to work on is yourself. You need to open your heart and say, "I'm ready. Give me a sign that this is the right path for me." Write it down. Shout it out. Whisper it, but *mean what you say, think, or write*—and it will happen.

Have you ever seen familiar shapes in clouds or looked at the ground and thought that the mere pattern of rocks feels familiar? There are scientific names for most of these habits, but to my spiritual heart, it means that I'm being sent a sign, which I'm open to receiving. It helps to familiarize yourself with different signs out there. They could be spirit animals, numbers, coincidental few words or situations, dreams, something you see on the street, or a piece of music you chance upon—again, when you open your heart, you'll be overwhelmed at just how much the universe is trying to show you. Acknowledge them, and work on acting based on how they make you feel. Use these signs to help you with crystal selection. When you combine your intuition with the wisdom of the universe, you open yourself up to limitless possibilities!

Have the Crystals and Supplies Been Ethically Sourced?

The next point to remember is to source your crystals ethically. I prefer buying crystals from local shops, but even if you get them online, try to chat with the store vendors before making your purchases. Some places don't follow fair wages and labor laws or respect indigenous communities when sourcing crystals or items for smoke cleansing. You don't want that kind of energy around you. Remember—the energies in your meditation items will also depend on the processes that go into their making. You don't need to surround yourself with any negative thought patterns, hurt, or grief. Even though we will cleanse these items before use, think of the people who were hurt in the process of obtaining them. That itself is a reason to be fully informed about what you let into your home and heart. Here are some questions you should consider:

- Are the people mining crystals compensated fairly?
- Are indigenous tribal practices being honored when mining or sourcing items?
- Are their working conditions alright, and are there safety mechanisms in place?
- Do the workers have protective equipment?
- What is the environmental impact of how these crystals are being sourced?
- Are there signs that child labor may be employed?

In most cases, the shops will be willing to help you out. But if someone gets angry or defensive when met with these questions, know this is a red flag. Try to look up reviews of the store online, or see if you can find a section where they describe their mining operations and places they source their stones. In some cases, it can be tough to find the answers you need. It's okay if this happens because you're going into it knowing you did the best you could. If possible, always choose shops and places where the answers are clear and direct.

Utilize Your Senses

Another great tip is to feel the crystal's aura. If you're unsure how to connect with a crystal physically, simply stroll through a crystal shop and see which ones capture your attention. Try working with moldavite, selenite, or shungite to test your sensitivity to crystals. These crystals have high vibrations that may evoke some sensation if you're receptive.

Experiment by hovering your hand a few centimeters above a crystal that catches your eye. I suggest using your left hand as it's believed that energy enters our body through the left side and exits through the right. Although not everyone is aware of this, most people tend to sense more with their left hand than their right (Hodges, 2020). Test each hand and see if you notice any differences.

While hovering your hand over the crystal, you may feel warmth, coldness, tingling, or pulsations in your palm. We're all unique, so we experience crystals in different ways. Generally, warmth indicates a physical effect, tingling suggests a spiritual connection, and coldness often relates to emotional or mental aspects.

If you're unsure whether you're feeling anything, try picking up the crystal and holding it gently in your left palm without closing your fingers around it. Give it a minute and observe if any sensations arise.

At this stage, some of us may experience tingling or a sensation traveling up our arms. We may feel the energy working elsewhere, targeting areas of imbalance. Crystals can stimulate our chakra system, resulting in feelings of light-headedness or a floating sensation. I often encounter emotions like joy, happiness, confidence, or strength when holding a crystal. Trust your own experiences and explore the profound connection between crystals and your unique being.

Finally (and this applies to all good things in life), take time and be patient. It will happen, I promise. But if you're getting overwhelmed, step back for a few minutes, realign yourself, and then return to your practice. It will always be there, waiting for you when you are ready.

We're getting close to the end. You've learned even more about crystals and how to choose the right ones for you. Following this sequence, in the next chapter, we talk about cleansing and programming your crystals—getting them ready for grid work.

CHAPTER 9

PREPARING YOUR CRYSTALS

I like to think of cleansing the same way I look at a cool shower after a long day of work on a hot day. I've come back carrying a plethora of energies from the outside. Not all of them are great. I'm tired and grumpy, and I could even be thinking that the world is messing with my head. Then, I step into the shower, let the cool water ease my senses, and tell me everything will be okay. After this, I can work with what I have with a cleaner intention. That's what cleansing does. It allows us to recharge and reprogram ourselves to better adapt to our circumstances.

CLEANSING AND PURIFYING CRYSTALS

Like humans, crystals have residual energies from the journey in which they are sourced, regardless of whether they're gifts or purchased. If we go to shops to buy them, many others pick them up like we do and transfer their energies into the stones. By the time we've purchased them, they're already carrying a lot of older energies— from other shop patrons, the miners, the store owners, and everything they've passed through between being formed and getting to you.

Plus, when we subject our crystals to repeated use, they work as magnets that draw our negative energies from our systems and the environment, leaving room for the positive ones. However, in doing so, they get depleted (Shine, 2018). They're working hard, and by not being in their natural environments occasionally, they may get malnourished over time. That's where cleansing and purifying comes in. It's like allowing your crystals to nourish themselves as you would nourish your body with water and food. The best way to do this is to simply attune your crystals to the natural environment.

Cleansing with the Elements

This is one of the simplest ways to cleanse your crystals. The elements of nature are naturally attuned to removing negative energies from your stone and helping it emit wholesome vibrations instead. When we learn meditation, we're often told to spend time in nature, connect our bare feet to the Earth, or let our eyes look at natural colors like green (Shine, 2018). This is because these activities rejuvenate us and help us reconnect with our roots. In the same way, the elements help crystals reconnect with their origins.

The first element is water. Choose natural water options as much as you can. This includes rainwater, ocean water, spring water, and so on. In countries like India, water is often collected from holy rivers like the Ganges and used for ritual practices later. Some crystals tend to be more porous and fragile and could get damaged easily, so be careful with them. Labradorite and azurite, for instance, don't do well if they're left submerged in water for too long. In general, raw stones are the most at risk, while tumbled and polished stones are usually safer with exposure to water. You may experiment by simply holding them under running water for a few seconds to see how they hold up, but if you are unsure and want to play it safe, there are plenty of other wonderful cleansing methods available. Some crystals can be cleaned with warm water and mild soap, but NEVER use boiling water. This could cause minerals in the stone to disintegrate. Plus, it's dangerous to work with something so abrasive.

To cleanse using water, simply hold your crystals under a stream or immerse them in a bowl for a few minutes. Visualize negative energies being washed away and replaced with uplifting, positive ones. After two to three minutes, pat your crystals dry with a soft cloth.

The next element, and the simplest cleansing agent, is air. All you need to do is leave the crystals out in the open, or you could even blow on them while thinking positive, cleansing thoughts. This will help negative energies dissipate. You can even use natural items like leaves, twigs, and feathers to wave air around or across the stone as you cleanse it.

Then, we have the element of earth, which will ground your crystal and pull any depleted, negative energies into the soil. It will replace these energies with positive, pure ones. To cleanse with this element, bury your crystal in the garden overnight or place it on top of a bowl of sand. Some stones could get brittle, so avoid using sand on softer crystals like moonstone, rhodochrosite, labradorite, and celestite. You can also use other related earthly elements, like leaving your crystal on a little flower pot with soil, over a rice bed, or in your herb garden.

Finally, we have fire. You can cleanse your crystals with smoke through a method called smudging by using lit incense, or you can briefly pass the stone through a candle flame. But remember to be careful when doing this, and don't burn yourself.

Smudging

To smudge your crystals, you will need smudging tools. These include dried herbs and plants like cedar and sage. Palo santo is revered for this practice, but be careful not to hurt indigenous communities if you work with this herb or even white sage. I've found that incense and herbs like rosemary work wonders as well. Choose herbs that align with your soul.

Prepare a fire-safe container like a ceramic bowl or an abalone shell (again, ensure this is ethically sourced) to catch embers and residues from burning herbs. Next, light the tip of the herb or your smudging tool and allow the flame to catch before gently blowing it out. You don't want a whole fire, just the healing smoke. Hold the tool over your container and allow the smoke to billow. Smudge yourself first, beginning from your head to your toes. Let the smoke envelope and purify your energies. Next, pass the crystals through the smoke to cleanse and recharge their energies.

Cleansing with the Sun and the Moon

Crystals and moonlight are the best of friends. A full moon is redolent with goddess energy, and a new moon has this same brilliance but softer. When left under the moonlight, your crystals experience deep energy cleansing (think of it as a deep tissue massage). Moonlight also fills your stones to the brim with loving and welcoming feminine vibrations ideal for nourishing your stones and your practice. A full moon comes with the energy of release, and a new one is all about growth (Tiny Rituals, 2023a). And just as you can cleanse your stones under the moonlight, so can you do it under sunlight. I prefer the early sun, which is not as harsh to invigorate my crystals and fill them with vibrant energy. The moon cleanses, and the sun recharges, so by the time early morning is done, you have a set of crystals that are completely ready for practice!

Cleansing your stones under moonlight and sunlight is a cakewalk. Simply keep them on your windowsill before bed and let them stay there overnight. I like to place my stones on windowsills at around seven in the evening and pick them back up at seven in the morning. Within these twelve hours, the healing and rejuvenating energies of the moon and the early sun work their wonders to cleanse my stones.

Moon cleansing is excellent for stones like selenite and labradorite that won't fare well if left too long in water. Don't worry if it's cloudy out there. Your crystals will heal and recharge all the same. In fact, if it's raining, you can leave water-safe crystals outside where they can experience the moon and the rain together—talk about double cleansing! Bonus points if you can leave it in a safe space in your garden to experience the added benefits of earth cleansing!

Another great way to cleanse your stones is during an eclipse, which represents a new chapter. It could be a solar or a lunar one. This is a great chance to fill your crystals with new energy. The lunar eclipse represents internal shifts and transitions, while the solar eclipse speaks to change and external shifts. If you feel your luck has been stagnant, cleansing your crystals by leaving them on a windowsill or in the open during an eclipse is a great way to invite new blessings into your life.

Cleansing with Other Crystals

Using other crystals like quartz to heal and cleanse your stones is great because some crystals act as natural healers, remove negative energies, and raise positive vibrations. If you work with quartz as a cleanser, ensure it is larger than the crystal you're cleansing. You can also work with smaller quartz crystals and place them on your altar or in a bowl. Then, let the healing energies of the quartz work on the other stones and clean your crystal's energy. After this, you can leave the cleansing stones to recharge under moonlight or smudge with incense for some added tender loving care.

Selenite is my favorite cleansing crystal because it heals both itself and other stones. You can use raw selenite or even opt for a selenite cleansing plate to purify and recharge your crystals. A cleansing plate is a flat platform that can be used to rest your crystals. They come in various shapes and sizes. Take advantage of the physical connection a cleansing plate offers! Allow them to rest for a day so they get entirely cleansed.

You can also go with the crystal points method. Choose your cleansing area and place a selenite or quartz tower in the center. Place the stones that need to be cleansed around the tower. This will heal and recharge all your crystals. If you'd like, you can keep separate selenite stones for cleansing and personal use.

Cleansing with Sound

Another beautiful and effective way to cleanse your stones is by using sound. Sound healing employs different vibrations, pitches, and tones to harmonize, cleanse, and amplify your crystals' innate energies. You can use instruments like tuning forks, singing bowls, or even your voice. A simple chant emits healing sound waves that envelop your crystals with restorative frequencies. These vibrations help release stagnant energy, align frequencies, and restore the natural balance of crystals. You only need to do this for a few minutes to thoroughly cleanse your crystals.

Cleansing with Breathwork

Breathwork is best for cleansing crystals of small size. For this to work, focus on your intentions and use quick exhalations to blow unwanted, negative energy away from the stones. Follow these steps:

1. Hold your crystal in your dominant hand (the hand you use for most work).
2. Take a deep breath in and focus on your intentions.
3. Exhale on your crystal with short, quick bursts of air.
4. Repeat this step for 30 seconds.
5. Allow the stone to shed all negative energies.

Cleansing with Visualization and Meditation

To cleanse your crystal using this technique, hold the crystal in your hand with a clear mind and heart. Visualize a radiant, healing light surrounding your crystal and permeating through it. Direct your thinking to picture impurities flushed out of your stone. Continue this process until you feel the crystal's energy balance has been restored.

Bonus Tip

For extra fragile crystals, you could rely on no-contact cleansing methods. For instance, if you want to water cleanse crystals that could be damaged with direct water contact, you can place a glass of water beside the crystal overnight and leave both on the windowsill to absorb the healing energies of the moon.

There's also a no-contact salt method. Fill a glass bowl about halfway with dry sea salt. Keep a smaller glass container or a drinking glass and press it so half of it is buried into this bowl in the salt, bottom side down. Then, keep your crystals in the second container or drinking glass so they can absorb the healing powers of the salt without the added abrasiveness. Once you've finished this (consider leaving the stones for one to two hours), discard the salt. This can also be used for other mediums, such as rice and soil.

Cleansing Multiple Crystals for Grids

You can cleanse surrounding and amplifying stones of the same type together or in batches. Gather them together and cleanse them as a group if desired, either by using the same cleansing method or individually. Not all crystal types can be purified in the same way, so check their compatibility beforehand. As for how frequently you should cleanse your crystals, a general guideline is to do it once a month. A cleansed and nourished crystal will exude bright, warm, and vibrant energy, which is very easy to connect and communicate with. You'll know when you're around it because it will beckon you with positive energies and be light to your touch. On the other hand, if a crystal feels heavy, static-like, and lacks flow, it may indicate that it requires cleansing to restore its optimal state.

PROGRAMMING YOUR CRYSTALS

After cleansing the crystals, program them to be entirely attuned to your intentions. Programming is a process that allows your crystal to carry your thoughts and intentions and sets its purpose. Our minds and bodies are connected, so when we program our crystals, we communicate our intentions from our minds to our physical cells and then transfer these intentions to the energy fields in the crystals (Ward, 2021). This tells our stones what we want them to do for us. It's a three-way bond between our souls, bodies, and crystals.

We connect deeper with ourselves, and by involving the stones in this purposeful activity, we channel our energies in a seamless back-and-forth exchange. Programming allows you to set your intentions on a clean slate and present these to your crystals so they know how to improve your life. For example, let's say I intend to release ties that no longer serve me and look for new love. In that case, I should choose crystals like rose quartz that amplify love and warm energies and feed my intentions into it.

Another way to program crystals is to place your stone on the corresponding chakra. Lie down on a mat or clean surface and simply keep your crystal on the chakra that resonates most with the intention of what you want to achieve (Ward, 2021). You can also keep the crystal on your third eye to tune into your psychic abilities and unleash your intuitive powers. When these intentions are set, you'll call on them again when you do your spellwork. With time, the process will become easier. **You don't need to program surrounding and amplifying stones**. Once you activate your grid, the intentions you programmed into your center stone will unify every stone together.

PUTTING IT ALL TOGETHER TO GET YOUR CRYSTALS READY FOR THE CRYSTAL GRID

To prepare your crystals for your grid, identify what you seek from crystal empowerment. This is your base intention, and it must be fed into your center stone. Choose your main center crystal, which will align with your core intention. If you are having trouble, go back to Chapter Seven once more and read which stones manifest which intentions.

Then, choose your surrounding crystals that can align with or complement the original intention by targeting different aspects to help you achieve the overall goal. For instance, if you want to work with financial abundance, you can keep citrine as a center stone for financial intentions and green aventurine as a surrounding stone to bring you more luck and abundance.

Seek harmony. Additional crystals should support, amplify, or target related characteristics that align with the core intention. Incorporate different shapes, combinations, or color magic based on what we learned—this is the time to get creative! You can even use other objects of importance to you.

Cleanse all your crystals and program your center crystal with your intention in mind. You can write the intention down if it helps. And with that, all the ingredients for your grid are ready.

In the next and final chapter, we go into greater detail about making your crystal grid with some examples, so once we're done, the world of crystal grid magic is ready to welcome you with open arms!

PART FOUR
SUPERCHARGE YOUR CRYSTALS THROUGH GRIDWORK

CHAPTER 10

4 SIMPLE STEPS TO CREATE YOUR CRYSTAL GRID

This chapter is all about building your crystal grid. Before we wrap up, I'll also share some recipes for pre-made crystal grids that you can implement for specific purposes!

HOW TO BUILD YOUR CRYSTAL GRID

There aren't any hard and fast rules for making a grid because it's an art form and an expression of your creative self. But you can follow some practices and guidelines to get the best out of your grid. Your grid's composition can be intuitive or structured. We'll go into the basic structural framework, how to build one by channeling your intuitions, and lastly, go over recipes you can use.

Before we move ahead, take a deep breath. This applies to when you actually make your grid as well. It is a ritual, and at the onset of any ritual, you want to set the mood by being in a calm, collected, and meditative state. Relax your breathing and count to ten in slow, measured breaths. You can set the ambiance with candles, incense, or meditative music.

Next, determine your grid's structure using what we learned about sacred geometry. Pick one symbol as your base shape. You can simply draw it on the floor, make it with dry rice grains, or print or paint it on cloth, wood, paper, or basically anything—the goal is to create a guide to help you visualize things better!

Follow all the steps we discussed at the end of Chapter Nine. After that, place your surrounding stones in the geometric shape you have in mind to build your grid. Be conscious of the distance between your crystals, and try to keep the spacing even. Also, take note of the direction in which energy is flowing.

Set your center stone down within the heart of your grid. If it helps you visualize the outcome, you can also write your intention down on a piece of paper and keep it under the center stone. Follow this by repeating the intention, either by saying it out loud or letting it resonate in your mind.

To activate your grid, hold fast to the intention in your mind. Take a crystal point, wand, or index finger and connect every individual surrounding crystal to the center stone, one at a time. If you need a refresher on how to activate crystal grids, review the section in Chapter Four.

Intuitive/Freeform Crystal Grids

If you're having trouble picking a grid structure or simply want to use your intuition to build a grid, here's what you can do. When creating the grid, lean into your intention and form the overall shape based on what feels right in your heart. A grid can be symmetrical or asymmetrical, but your intuition must be clear. Additionally, you can have circular, triangular, vertical, cross-shaped, rectangular grids, or any shape that speaks to your soul. The shape can be as simple or complex as you want. You are not in competition with anyone, so do what feels best for your purpose. This is also a great time to try building a grid based on the shapes you experienced in the world and/or drew in your sketchbook (as discussed in Chapter Two). You want the experience to be rewarding, so let your creativity roam free.

MAINTAINING YOUR CRYSTAL GRID

To maintain the connection with your crystal grid, you have to meditate with it. Visualize your intention when doing so, and picture what it feels like to have the life and outcome you dream of come true. You can wire-wrap the crystal grid together and hang it up on the wall or simply let it remain where it is. Give a week to reaffirm your intentions by meditating and visualizing. From there, you can decide whether you'd like to deconstruct your grid, cleanse, and use the crystals for something else.

If you need to cleanse your grid without deconstructing it, you can simply place a selenite or quartz crystal near your grid, smudge over it, or use your breath over your stones. If possible, make your grid near a window so the natural moon and sun cycles can keep replenishing your grid's energy.

If you have a mobile, wire-wrapped grid that can be taken to different environments, consider leaving it out when it rains or taking it to the garden for some time to cleanse it in nature. After you do this, you may want to reprogram your center crystal with your intentions and activate the grid again.

CRYSTAL GRID RECIPES

Now that you know how to create your own grids, here are some model grids that you can follow or simply derive inspiration from! We'll start off with an easy—but no less effective—amplification grid.

A Simple Starter Amplification Grid

This easy grid will be ready in a jiffy and work beautifully to amplify your intentions. You'll need the following:

- three clear quartz crystals
- one center stone with a meaning aligned with your intentions

Shape the three clear quartz crystals in a triangle. Then, program your center stone and place it in the heart of this triangle. That's all you need to do! Next, you can simply activate your grid. Clear quartz is great because it's a powerful amplifier.

Now, let's go over some recipes for crystal grid spells that could be useful for your practice. Note that these recipes may have multiple options, allowing you the freedom to choose what you feel is best for your current situation.

A Grid for Prosperity

Be it abundance, health, or anything that fills your cup with happiness, everyone deserves prosperity in their lives.

Grid Structure: the flower of life

Center Stone: citrine, pyrite, tiger's eye, or emerald

Surrounding Stones: any of the above, green aventurine, green jade, and clear quartz

Ideas for Objects of Importance: rings, coins, dollar bills, pictures from your vision board, postcards for places you'd like to visit, travel souvenirs

Procedure:

1. Begin by cleansing your space and your crystals. You need to cleanse and prepare your crystals at least a day in advance so they have enough time to

rest and be ready to receive new energy. Cleanse the space where you will have your crystal grid. You can smudge it or use sound healing to give it a sound bath. That way, any stagnant or negative energy in the space will be removed.

2. Just like how you prepare your surroundings, also prepare yourself. Take a relaxing bath and listen to some meditative music beforehand. You should be completely calm and focused on your intention of prosperity before you begin. Reflect on what prosperity means to you, touch your crystals, and ensure they feel right for your purpose.

3. Set an affirmation that amplifies this intention in the present tense. An example is: "I am becoming richer every day."

4. Program your center stone with this intention before setting it down. Then, make the sacred geometry shape with the surrounding stones and objects. If a flower of life feels complicated at the onset, a triangle or a square will also work just the same kind of wonders. Remember, intention before all.

5. Plan your grid's direction. The surrounding stones can point inward to the center stone or outward. The former indicates you wish yourself an inward flow of prosperity, and the latter means you want prosperity for others in your life. Fix the direction based on this.

6. Place your center stone in the middle with your intention in mind.

7. Once your stones are in place, activate your grid by moving a selenite wand or your index finger from the center stone to each surrounding stone. Move back up to the center stone from the surrounding one, return to that same stone, and then go clockwise to the next one. Follow this pattern until you've covered all surrounding stones, and remember your intention throughout the process.

A Grid for Love

We all go through periods of emotional stagnancy when it feels like we have so much love to give, yet none of it is coming back to us. When this happens, a love manifestation grid could become the key to getting the right kind of attraction flowing and imbuing some chemistry into our lives! This grid could also help you heal from past relationships, improve current ones, or simply become a conduit for a healthy serving of self-love.

Grid Structure: a heart shape (represents the union of two complete circles), a triangle works for this as well!

Center Stone: rose quartz (hands down)

Surrounding Stones: pink opal, clear quartz, selenite, and rhodonite (tip: you can use clear quartz in all grids because this lovely crystal will always amplify your intention)

Ideas for Objects of Importance: jewelry (like necklaces or bracelets), tarot cards, rose petals, additionally you could light a soothing scented candle and place it within your grid (have it lit during the initial activation, then for subsequent meditation sessions)

Procedure:

1. Cleanse your space, crystals, and self before building your grid.
2. Think about your priority in terms of love and write it down in a present-tense affirmation—like you're already experiencing it. For instance, you could write, "I am in a loving, healthy relationship that fulfills me in every way." Add an amplifying sentence. A good option is, "This manifests and comes true easily because it is for my highest good."
3. Program your intention into the center rose quartz. To do this, hold the crystal in your dominant hand and repeat the intention or affirmation eight to 12 times or until you feel a shift in your energy. It could be something as subtle as feeling a little spark come alive.
4. Place your surrounding stones in a heart shape (or triangle) and the center stone in the middle with your intention in mind. For added wholesome energy, I like to arrange more amplification stones and items of personal value in a little circle

between the center stone and the outer shape (this is optional).

5. Take your index finger or selenite wand and activate your grid by moving from the center stone to each surrounding stone. Repeat your intention and affirmations, and let them fill the stones and the space with sacred energy.

A Grid for Spiritual Awakening

Spiritual awakening is essential for all of us because, without it, we go through life like automatons, unaware of any deeper purpose to our existence. This can manifest in unhappiness, even depression. Spiritual awakening helps us connect with our higher selves and attune ourselves to the healing, grounding energy of the world around us.

Grid Structure: a circle or spiral

Center Stone: amethyst

Surrounding Stones: clear quartz, moonstone, selenite, and labradorite

Ideas for Objects of Importance: tarot cards, prayer beads, anything that represents and helps you connect with your spirit guides, additionally you could light incense for the initial activation and subsequent meditation sessions

Procedure:

1. Cleanse your space, crystals, and yourself.
2. Set your grid's intention and focus on inner growth, connection with higher consciousness, and overall spiritual awakening.
3. Set an affirmation in tune with your intention, like "I can hear the voice of my higher conscience," and program your center stone with this.
4. Arrange the surrounding stones in a circle or spiral pattern, and place your center amethyst in the heart of this pattern with your intention in mind.
5. While placing the stones, visualize, affirm, and, if necessary, repeat your intentions out loud. See yourself expanding in consciousness and embracing the incoming inner wisdom.
6. If you desire, place additional items like symbols, candles, or personal effects around your grid.
7. Activate your grid by moving from the center stone to each of the surrounding stones. Once you reach the surrounding stone, move back up to the center stone, return to this stone, and then move clockwise to the next one. Repeat this until you cover all the crystals. Keep your intention in mind throughout this process.

A Grid for Emotional Healing

This grid is perfect for when you're feeling emotionally blocked, hurt, or anxious. It is ideal for balancing your heart chakra and filling your soul and spirit with warm, compassionate, and forgiving energy.

Grid Structure: a seed of life or a square shape

Center Stones: rose quartz or rhodonite

Surrounding Stones: amethyst, amazonite, blue lace agate, and pink opal

Ideas for Objects of Importance: items from nature, journal pages, or any mementos that bring you joy and happiness

Procedure:

1. The day before, engage in an evening of self-care. This could include activities such as curling up on the couch with your favorite novel and a hot cup of tea or visiting the spa.
2. Cleanse your stones, space, and yourself.
3. Prepare your intention beforehand, and manifest it in the form of an affirmation that is true in the present tense. An example is "I am no longer trapped by hate."
4. Program your center crystal with your intention.

5. Set the surrounding stones in the pattern you choose, and place the center crystal in the heart of this pattern with your intention in mind.

6. Activate your grid by moving your index finger or wand from the center stone to each surrounding stone. Suffuse the stone with your intention, travel back up to the center stone, then back down, and move clockwise to the next surrounding stone in the grid. Do this until each crystal embodies what you intend.

A Grid for Wellness

Wellness forms the core of a fulfilling, healthy, and balanced life. It encompasses emotional, mental, physical, and spiritual well-being. When you prioritize it, you focus on maintaining harmony both within and around you. You pay attention to nurturing yourself on all levels and approach life with a view that is always geared toward abundance.

Grid Structure: a circle

Center Stone: amethyst or clear quartz

Surrounding Stones: rose quartz, citrine, and green aventurine

Ideas for Objects of Importance: small house plants, acorns, leaves, skipping stones, candles, your favorite incense sticks

Procedure:

1. Go for a long walk and reflect on your life. Think about a clear focus for your grid intention.
2. Cleanse your space, self, and crystals.
3. Set your intention for the grid. Write the intention down as an affirmation happening right now. An example could be, "I am healthy, vital, and energized."
4. Program your center stone with your intention.
5. Set your surrounding stones in a circle shape, and place your center stone in the heart of this circle.
6. Activate the grid by moving your wand or index finger from the center stone to each surrounding stone, back up, back down, and clockwise to the next stone. Repeat until you've covered all the stones and infused them with your intention.

Bonus Tip: For that extra boost (works for any grid), activation during a new moon always helps because it infuses your grids with the power of new beginnings.

Bonus Grid to Protect Your Home

This grid works wonders for shielding your entire home and family from negative or stagnant energy. It is also excellent for opening your mind to the possibilities of how to use crystal grids and what they can achieve! To make this grid, follow these steps:

1. Source black tourmaline and selenite. Cleanse each of the crystals.

2. Set your intention with a positive affirmation like, "This grid protects me and my family energetically."

3. For this grid, program your intention into each of the crystals. Here's a quick calculation of how many crystals you'll need:

   a. One selenite for each of your walls, doorways, and windows (the purpose of the selenite is to connect the tourmalines).

   b. One tourmaline in the corners of the outermost rooms of your home (So, if your home's outer spaces are a living room, study, or balcony, you'll need one tourmaline for each corner of these spaces. The tourmaline sets up a protective boundary for energies, and the selenite cleanses and purifies existing energy.)

4. Activate your grid by beginning where it feels most natural. Many of us like to do this by starting from a crystal in the northernmost part of the room.

5. Move around your home from one crystal to the next in a clockwise motion and draw energy connections (visualize them as strings of white light) from one stone to the next. Do this with a wand or your index finger.

6. Once you connect all the stones, you have your

harmonious home protection grid! Remember to cleanse these stones at least once a month.

ADDITIONAL TIPS

If you're just starting out or looking for something simple, look for basic shapes and focus hard on your intention. Don't be intimidated by elaborate grids or put off by what you make. What looks unattractive to you could be just what you need, so long as your intention is clear and infused into your grid.

The most important thing is your center crystal and ensuring it aligns with your intentions. Remember, the law of attraction is true and universal—*you get back more of what you put out into the world, so keep it simple, healthy, and clean.* Once every few days, meditate near your grid to affirm your intentions. Feel the comfort and safety of your personal ritual space. Bask in the positive energies that envelope and nourish you. Trust me; you'll emerge feeling like a new and happier version of yourself each time. And always keep your crystals away from any unwanted energies—from the get-go if you can!

MANAGING EXPECTATIONS

Another great little thing to remember is that your crystals will work with and amplify what already exists, so when you begin your gridwork, the two first steps should always be cleansing your space and yourself. Set the intentions you want to achieve, and know you will attract them because *it is what you are seeking*. And as Rumi once said, "What you seek is seeking you."

Manifesting is an ongoing journey; every journey is best enjoyed only when you're truly involved in the little things along the way. So enjoy the experience, and let your grid help you. Give things time, trust the process, and stick with it. We all have unique energies, so never compare the first chapter of your book to the last chapter of someone else's. Your grid will always work best when you are grounded, so, dear reader,

Believe.
Believe.
Believe.

With that, we've reached the end of our journey together. I'll take a few more minutes of your time and wrap up at the turn of a page!

CONCLUSION

Here we are, at the end of this journey and the beginning of your foray into the world of crystal grids. As someone going into this with the very intention of improving life, know you've already started off on the right foot. Listen to the world's signs and your own heart, and you will never go wrong.

Throughout our journey together in this book, we learned all about crystals, their histories, color magic, sacred geometry, grid creation, and amplifying your intentions with these grids. With all the information you now have, you're ready to go out, get your own little kit, cleanse it, and begin your foray into healing and rejuvenation. You can hunt for more grid shapes and spells for other intentions if you wish.

I'd like to end with what I know about crystal healing. When I started my journey, I had no idea how much the world around me could influence my energies. I'd heard abstract concepts, but none made sense until I began using crystals and discovered just how much I was holding inside of me.

With each crystal, it felt as if I could let go of the negatives and invite something more positive, healing, and nourishing into my life. It opened my eyes to the world of energy healing and made me realize that we are all interconnected particles to one cosmic whole.

I hope you enjoyed coming on this journey with me and that each new thing you learned will help you on the way to manifesting and creating the life you've always dreamed of having. Never feel as though it is selfish to desire abundance and good things in your life.

Never guilt yourself into thinking you're not worthy enough or that bad things happen because you deserve them. No. You deserve sunshine and window seats by the rain, walks in mossy forests and hot cups of tea, hearts full of love, and heads full of good dreams. And when you intend to fill your life with them, *every day becomes more of what you want.*

Your crystals and grids will only help you set this life in motion.

You, yourself, will make it a reality.

Ready to Illuminate the Path for Others?

No matter where we stand on our spiritual journey, we all seek guidance, and your insights can make all the difference.

Your honest opinion about this book on Amazon could be the beacon someone needs to unlock their inner power and explore the remarkable strength of crystal grids.

Your support means the world to me, and I'm confident that countless others will be grateful too. Our individual energy is potent, but when shared, it becomes an unstoppable force.

Visit the link below or scan the QR code to leave your review on Amazon.

https://cosmiccompendiums.com/review

I can't wait to hear about your personal experiences with grids and what you achieved with them. Thank you for being a guiding light!

REFERENCES

Abouzelof, J. (2018, May). *Iolite Meaning: Healing Properties & Everyday Uses*. Tinyrituals.co. https://tinyrituals.co/blogs/tiny-rituals/iolite-meaning-healing-properties-everyday-uses

Abouzelof, J. (2022, February 5). *Merlinite Meaning*. Moonrise Crystals. https://moonrisecrystals.com/merlinite-meaning/#:

Ahmad, S. (2021, February 25). *Healing Third Eye Chakra Migraine*. Success Consciousness. https://www.successconsciousness.com/blog/wellness/healing-third-eye-chakra-migraine/

Anahana. (2022, October 17). *Chakra Stones And Chakra Crystals - Meaning, How to Use*. https://www.anahana.com/en/yoga/chakra-stones-and-chakra-crystals

Anahana. (2023). *Red Jasper - Stone, Meaning, Properties, Benefits, Bracelet*. https://www.anahana.com/en/lifestyle/crystals/red-jasper

Asana. (2022, March 5). *Purple Gemstones | All Purple Crystal Types, Meanings, Names*. https://crystal-shop.co/purple-gemstones/

Beadnova. (2020, July 7). *Yellow Crystals and Stones List: Names, Meaning, Healing, and Uses*. https://www.beadnova.com/blog/14260/yellow-crystal-stones

Better Sleep. (2022, December 9). *Opening the Crown Chakra*. https://www.bettersleep.com/blog/opening-the-crown-chakra/

Bibleinfo. (n.d.). *What Does the Bible Say About Crystals?* https://www.bibleinfo.com/en/questions/what-does-bible-say-about-crystals

BlackTreeLab. (2023). *Gemstones in Buddhism: Setting the Facts Straight*. https://blacktreelab.co/blogs/news/gemstones-in-buddhism-setting-the-facts-straight

Borates Today. (2022, August 12). *Howlite Crystal For Calming and Positive Energy*. https://borates.today/howlite-crystal-for-calming-and-positive-energy/

Brahma Gems. (2023, April 13). *Can Ruby Increase Blood Circulation: Health Benefits of Ruby Gemstone*. Brahma Gems. https://brahmagems.com/blog/can-ruby-increase-blood-circulation-health-benefits-of-ruby-gemstone.html

Camille. (2021, April 16). *12 Healing Crystals for Migraines And*

Headaches. Crystal Healing Ritual. https://www.crystalhealingritual.com/crystals-for-migraines/

Cape Cod Crystals. (2023). *The Meaning of Black Crystals and Stones | Black Color Meaning.* https://capecodcrystals.com/pages/black-crystal-meaning

Charms of Light. (2023a). *Tanzanite Healing Properties | Tanzanite Meaning | Benefits Of Tanzanite | Metaphysical Properties Of Tanzanite.* Charms Of Light. https://www.charmsoflight.com/tanzanite-healing-properties

Charms of Light. (2023b). *Kyanite Healing Properties | Kyanite Meaning | Benefits Of Kyanite | Metaphysical Properties Of Kyanite.* https://www.charmsoflight.com/kyanite-healing-properties

Charms of Light. (2023c). *Turquoise Healing Properties | Turquoise Meaning | Benefits Of Turquoise | Metaphysical Properties Of Turquoise.* Charms Of Light. https://www.charmsoflight.com/turquoise-healing-properties

Chee, C. (2021a, August 12). *What is Kunzite? Properties & Everyday Uses of This Precious Pink Stone.* Truly Experiences Blog. https://trulyexperiences.com/blog/kunzite-gemstone/

Chee, C. (2021b, September 27). *All About Unakite Stone: Meaning & Healing Properties.* Truly Experiences Blog. https://trulyexperiences.com/blog/unakite-stone/

Cho, A. (2022a, August 25). *The Use and Meaning of Topaz Gemstone.* The Spruce. https://www.thespruce.com/topaz-feng-shui-properties-4151695

Cho, A. (2022b, August 31). *How You Can Use Jade in Feng Shui.* The Spruce. https://www.thespruce.com/jade-meaning-ancient-strength-and-serenity-1274373#:

Crystal Rock Star. (2017, December 5). *Nuummite - The 3 Billion Year Old Protection Crystal.* https://blog.crystalrockstar.com/nuummite/

Crystal Vaults. (2023a). *Creedite Healing Properties, Meanings, and Uses.* https://www.crystalvaults.com/crystal-encyclopedia/creedite/

Crystal Vaults. (2023b). *Hiddenite Healing Properties, Meanings, and Uses.* https://www.crystalvaults.com/crystal-encyclopedia/hiddenite/

Crystal Vaults. (2023c). *Rosasite Healing Properties, Meanings, and Uses.* https://www.crystalvaults.com/crystal-encyclopedia/rosasite/

Crystals & Holistic Healing. (n.d.). *Larimar - Metaphysical Healing Properties.* https://www.healingwithcrystals.net.au/larimar.html

Davis, F. (2021a, February 1). *How Ancient Cultures Used Crystals & What We Can Learn from Them*. Cosmic Cuts. https://cosmiccuts.com/blogs/healing-stones-blog/ancient-cultures-and-crystals

Davis, F. (2021b, May 2). *17 Native American Gemstones to Bring You Closer to the Earth*. Cosmic Cuts. https://cosmiccuts.com/blogs/healing-stones-blog/native-american-gemstones

Davis, F. (2022, March 17). *Black Onyx Healing Properties: Your Ultimate Spiritual Protection Crystal*. Cosmic Cuts. https://cosmiccuts.com/en-ae/blogs/healing-stones-blog/black-onyx-healing-properties

Energy Muse. (2022, September 19). *6 Pink Stones to Remedy All Matters of the Heart*. https://energymuse.com/blogs/crystals/pink-crystals

Gaia. (2020, November 6). *Do You Know the Meaning and Benefits of the Shri Yantra?* https://www.gaia.com/article/what-is-the-power-of-shri-yantra

Galo, G. (2023, April 13). *Ultimate Guide to Obsidian Crystal: Meanings, Properties, Facts and More*. Truly Experiences Blog. https://trulyexperiences.com/blog/obsidian-crystal/

Gemporia. (2018, July 2). *The Most Treasured Gemstones of Ancient Egypt and Ancient China*. https://www.gemporia.com/en-us/gemology-hub/article/990/the-most-treasured-gemstones-of-ancient-egypt-and-ancient-china/

Gem Pundit. (2022, January 29). *Healing Properties and Benefits of Malachite*. https://www.gempundit.com/blog/malachite-stone-uses-meaning-and-healing-properties

HealCrystal. (2023, March 30). *Natural Stones for High Blood Pressure*. https://healcrystal.com/prescriptions/diseases/natural-stones-for-high-blood-pressure/

Healing Crystals. (2010, November 3). *Crystals to Help with Bone Issues*. https://www.healingcrystals.com/Crystals_to_help_with_Bone_Issues_Articles_1927.html

Healing Energy Rocks. (2021, April 23). *Hematite - An Iron Stone for Blood Circulation, the Mind & Kind Love*. https://www.healingenergyrocks.com/post/healing-crystals-hematite

Healing with Crystals. (n.d.). *Vanadinite - Metaphysical Healing Properties Healing Crystal*. https://www.healingwithcrystals.net.au/vanadinite.html

Hoare, K. (2020, December 30). *How to Balance Your Chakra for Digestion*. Nutritionist Resource. https://www.nutritionist-resource.

org.uk/blog/2020/12/30/how-to-balance-your-chakra-for-digestion

Hodges, K. (2020, July 1). *How to Feel and Choose a Crystal*. Serendipity Crystals. https://serendipitycrystals.co.uk/how-to-feel-and-choose-a-crystal

Le Comptoir Geologique. (n.d.). *Lithotherapy - Silver Obsidian*. https://www.le-comptoir-geologique.com/metaphysicals-silver-obsidian.html

May, A. (2022, January 14). *Garnet Stone Benefits | Learn Garnet Stone Meaning*. Azeera. https://www.azeera.com/blog/the-art-of-gems/gemstones-in-astrology-garnet

McKinnon, L. (2021, August 10). *How to Use a Crystal Grid*. Drops-of-Gratitude. https://www.dropsofgratitude.ca/post/crystalgrid

Medlicott, C. (2019, October 8). *Crystals Of Ancient Egypt*. Mystical One. https://www.mysticalone.com/blog/crystals-of-ancient-egypt

MyCrystals. (n.d.). *Red Crystals*. https://www.mycrystals.com/color/red-crystals

Nast, C. (2020, December 29). *Would You Use Crystals to Help Conception? Everything You Need to Know About Fertility Crystals and Why Everyone's Searching For Them*. Glamour UK. https://www.glamourmagazine.co.uk/article/what-are-fertility-crystals

Navratan. (2022). *Enticing Garnet Stone Benefits & Healing Properties*. https://www.navratan.com/blog/garnet-stone-benefits

Nguyen, J. (2023, February 22). *Working With This Sacred, Ancient Symbol Can Foster Balance & Unity*. Mindbodygreen. https://www.mindbodygreen.com/articles/flower-of-life-meaning

Nunez, K. (2020, September 3). *Shungite Stone: Healing Properties, Benefits, Uses, More*. Healthline. https://www.healthline.com/health/shungite#how-to-use

Oakes, L. (n.d.). *Sunstone Aids SAD Seasonal Affective Disorder*. Healing-CrystalsForYou.com. Retrieved May 29, 2023, from https://www.healing-crystals-for-you.com/sunstone.html

Oriental Healing Oasis. (2023). *Gemstone & Crystal Therapy | Oriental Healing Oasis & Wellness Center*. https://orientalhealingoasis.com/gemstone-crystal-therapy

Pacinello, N. (2011, September 18). *The 10 Most Effective Crystals for Emotional Balance & How They Work*. The Crystal Cavern. https://

thecrystalcavernshop.com/blogs/news/crystals-for-emotional-balance

Pathak, P. (2015, Winter 3). *What's the Significance of Gemstones in Islam?* Speakingtree. https://www.speakingtree.in/allslides/the-signifi cance-of-gemstones-in-islam/263053

Rare Earth Gallery (n.d.). *Crystal Shapes: Their Meanings and Uses.* https://www.rareearthgallerycc.com/blog-entry/84/crystal-shapes:-their-meanings-and-uses

Regan, S. (2021, April 20). *The Spiritual Meaning of Shapes: A Glimpse Into Sacred Geometry + How To Use It.* Mindbodygreen. https://www.mindbodygreen.com/articles/sacred-geometry

Reiki Crystal Products (2022). *Natural Pyrite Stone Benefits & Use.* https://www.reikicrystalproducts.com/blog/post/natural-pyrite-stone-benefits-use

Rekstis, E. (2018, June 21). *Healing Crystals 101.* Healthline; Healthline Media. https://www.healthline.com/health/mental-health/guide-to-healing-crystals

Ress, J. (n.d.). *How To Use the Healing Powers of Quartz Crystals.* SpaGoddess Apothecary. https://spagoddess.com/blogs/spagod dess-wellness-blog/clear-quartz-crystals

Rosebud Woman. (2021, February 25). *Creating a Personal Ritual Space.* https://rosewoman.com/blogs/perspectives/sacred-spaces-in-everyday-life

Rudraksha Ratna. (n.d.). *White Zircon Gemstone Meaning, Benefits of White Zircon.* https://www.rudraksha-ratna.com/articles/white-zircon-gemstones

Saint Thomas, S. (2018, September 25). *Color Magic: A Witch's Guide to Color Meanings and Energies.* Allure; Allure. https://www.allure.com/story/color-magic-witchcraft-meanings-guide

Satin Crystals. (2023). *Top 5 Popular Green Healing Crystals - Using Gemstones & Color.* https://satincrystals.com/pages/the-color-green-meaning-crystal-healing-cultural-significance

Shine, T. (2018). *How to Cleanse, Charge, and Activate Healing Crystals.* Healthline. https://www.healthline.com/health/how-to-cleanse-crystals

Shubhanjali. (2022, August 20). *Introduction of Blue Crystals, Health Benefits, Healing Properties | Use Blue Crystal.* https://shubhanjalis

tore.com/introduction-of-blue-crystals-health-benefits-healing-properties/

Sipos, E. (2023, February 26). *How Peridot Can Enhance Your Well-Being*. AOV Crystals. https://aovcrystals.com/how-peridot-can-enhance-your-well-being/

Springsteen, B. (n.d.). *Rhodonite - Metaphysical Healing Properties*. CRYSTALS & HOLISTIC HEALING. Retrieved May 28, 2023, from https://www.healingwithcrystals.net.au/rhodonite.html

Springsteen, B. (2023). *Tiger Eye - Metaphysical Healing Properties*. CRYSTALS & HOLISTIC HEALING. https://www.healingwithcrystals.net.au/tiger-eye.html

Stelter, G. (2016, October 4). *A Beginner's Guide to the 7 Chakras and Their Meanings*. Healthline. https://www.healthline.com/health/fitness-exercise/7-chakras

Sugarman, A. (2021, April 27). *The Throat Chakra or Vishuddha*. Ekhart Yoga. https://www.ekhartyoga.com/articles/practice/throat-chakra-or-vishuddha

Supriya, A. (2022, August 1). *Blue Sapphire - A Miraculous Stone To Bring Instant Positivity In Life | Dharma-WeRIndia*. Dharma. https://dharma.werindia.com/blue-sapphire-a-miraculous-stone-to-bring-instant-positivity-in-life/

Terragni Consulting. (2023). *Labradorite Healing Properties*. https://terragni.in/bd05ho/labradorite-healing-properties

Times of India. (2019, December 25). *3 Crystals That Work for Weight Loss*. https://m.timesofindia.com/life-style/health-fitness/home-remedies/3-crystals-that-work-for-weight-loss/photostory/72953082.cms#:

Tiny Rituals. (2023a). *How To Cleanse Crystals: 9 Crucial Practices You Need To Know*. https://tinyrituals.co/blogs/tiny-rituals/how-to-cleanse-crystals

Tiny Rituals. (2023b). *Kunzite Meaning: Healing Properties & Everyday Uses*. https://tinyrituals.co/blogs/tiny-rituals/kunzite-meaning-healing-properties-everyday-uses

Tiny Rituals. (2023c). *Moldavite Meaning: Physical, Mental, & Spiritual Benefits*. https://tinyrituals.co/blogs/tiny-rituals/moldavite-meaning

Tiny Rituals. (2023d). *Opal Meaning: Healing Properties, Uses, & Benefits*. https://tinyrituals.co/blogs/tiny-rituals/opal-meaning

Tiny Rituals. (2023e). *Sugilite Meaning- Physical, Mental, & Spiritual Healing Properties.* https://tinyrituals.co/blogs/tiny-rituals/sugilite-meaning

Tiny Rituals. (2023f). *White Crystals: Healing Properties, Uses, & Benefits.* https://tinyrituals.co/blogs/tiny-rituals/white-crystal

Trikaya | Buddhism. (2019). In *Encyclopædia Britannica.* https://www.britannica.com/topic/trikaya

Truly Experiences Blog. (2021, September 27). *10 Best Crystals for Money: Stones to Attract Wealth & Prosperity.* https://trulyexperiences.com/blog/crystals-for-money/

Vinader, M. (2005). *Amethyst in Ancient Greece.* Monica Vinader. https://www.monicavinader.com/blog/gemstones/amethyst/amethyst-in-ancient-greece

Ward, K. (2021, February 17). *How to Cleanse and Charge Your Crystals, Because That's Something You Should Do.* Cosmopolitan. https://www.cosmopolitan.com/lifestyle/a32097392/how-to-cleanse-crystals/

Yoga Journal. (2021, March 12). *Intro to the Fourth Chakra: Heart Chakra (Anahata) | Subtle Body.* https://www.yogajournal.com/yoga-101/chakras-yoga-for-beginners/intro-heart-chakra-anahata/

Young, O. (2021, July 17). *Black Tourmaline's Meaning, Properties, and Healing Benefits.* Conscious Items. https://consciousitems.com/blogs/crystal-guides/black-tourmaline-meaning-properties

Young, O. (2022, April 22). *Orange Crystals: The 20 Stones for Manifesting, Creativity and Power.* Conscious Items. https://consciousitems.com/blogs/practice/orange-crystals